INGREDIENTS
OF
YOUNG OUTLIERS

ACHIEVING YOUR MOST AMAZING FUTURE

JOHN SHUFELDT, MD, JD, MBA

Inquiries should be addressed to:
Outliers Publishing
7332 E. Butherus Drive
Scottsdale, AZ 85260

Although the author and publisher have made every effort to ensure that the information in this book was correct at press time, the author and publisher do not assume and hereby disclaim any liability to any party for any loss, damage, or disruption caused by errors or omissions, whether such errors or omissions result from negligence, accident, or any other cause. Additionally, the author would like to thank the copyright holders included in this book for their contribution to this work.

ISBN Paperback: 978-1-940288-04-8

ISBN Hardcover 978-1-940288-05-5

ISBN Ebook: 978-1-940288-06-2

Printed in the United States of America

Cover design by Slobodan Cedic

Interior design and layout by Perfect Bound Marketing + Press

Manuscript review by Bob Kelly of WordCrafters, Inc.

*To our children Michael and Kaleigh,
who are the individuals I wanted to be
at their age. Thank you for teaching and
inspiring me every day!*

*To Dr. Barbara Duncan for her amazing
ability to educate the next group of Outliers,
for giving me the idea for this book and for
editing the first version.*

*To Brenda Rico and her fifth grade class,
whose excitement energized the efforts and
inspired the content in this book!*

August 30, 2013

Dear Dr. Shufeldt,

I absoulotely loved your talk. It was very fun to meet an author in person. also I can't wait for your leadership book for kids. You are a very good role model to everyone. My favorite part of the day is when Mrs. Rico reads your book to us and we get to hac some quotes and stories. I am a better version of my self because of your talk. I liked all the quotes that you had talked about and stories you had shared. Thank you lots!.

Your friend,
Sophia

To Sophia for making my day!

TABLE OF CONTENTS

INTRODUCTION

Each of us is created in a unique way. Our personalities are as diverse as the universe itself. Yet there is one constant: We can, by using what we have to the fullest, stand out from the crowd.
~ Glenn Van Ekeren

I was recently invited to Brenda Rico's class at Finley Farms School to talk about what it takes to become an outlier. Her students were smart, attentive, and very well mannered – clearly a group of early outliers. I asked them for some advice on how to get others motivated to read this book. They had some great ideas: billboards; celebrity endorsements; radio spots; print ads; and social media – to name just a few. As Mrs. Rico pointed out, "They were a lot more hip" than she and I were at their age!

A day after the presentation, I received a copy of a letter from Sophia, one of the students in the class. In it, she wrote, "I am a better version of myself because of your talk." To date, I've received no greater praise or reward after any talk than that one sentence from Sophia.

I've often wondered why some young people struggle so much and what makes others – like Sophia and others in Mrs. Rico's class – ready and able to change the world. Is it simply from parents, friends, and role models along the way? Teachers and mentors provide the education and support, thereby allowing us to look "just over the horizon" and view potential futures. I still track down some of my former teachers and get great satisfaction out of thanking them. Without their influence, I'd be less educated and less motivated than the person I am today.

Parents and siblings offer the unconditional love necessary for us to venture outside our comfort zone to dare, explore, and risk. Good parents raise children who'll make the world a better place. Friends and classmates afford the encouragement, support, and sometimes labor, allowing us leverage our vision.

My experience in Mrs. Rico's class inspired me to spend some time thinking back to my own pre-college days, particularly after making the trek back to my 35th high school class reunion. Class reunions, no matter how long ago the graduation, are a fantastic opportunity to observe the diversity of paths and outcomes among your former peer group.

Some of our class "superstars" made the post-high school transition without any difficulty. Others struggled for years along their path. Thirty-five years later, a few are still struggling, and will probably never become the person they once hoped to be.

What makes someone a standout – an outlier? What ingredients make outliers unique? And where can the rest of us find those ingredients? Thus began my search to find that "secret sauce," those special ingredients in the recipe which when combined make an individual an outlier.

I'm getting a bit old – at least that's what my kids tell me. Along my journey, I've had some fantastic experiences and met some amazing people who taught me, again and again, that we all have the necessary ingredients to become outliers – we just need to remember them.

The people I've met or cared for as a physician have come from all walks of life, from different ethnicities, and from varied educational and religious backgrounds. Some have taught me how to conduct myself. Others have taught me exactly how *not* to conduct myself. I've learned something from each of them and appreciate all the lessons.

I was adopted from an orphanage before my memory took hold. My parents were hard working, loving, strict, and honest. They gave me every opportunity imaginable and supported my older sister and me as best they knew how.

The one thing I lacked, and would change if I could, is that I wasn't fortunate enough to be introduced to a mentor – someone who would have opened doors, kicked me in the rear end, or patted me on the back, as necessary. In the Navy, this role is called a Sea Daddy – someone who takes a less-experienced crewmember under his or her wing and provides expert tutelage.

I take complete responsibility for my lack of a mentor; I simply didn't put myself out there to investigate the possibilities of what a mentor could do to help me. Consequently, I was my own best and worst counsel. Subsequently, I made lots of mistakes along the way. Persevering through these mistakes, and reading books, as well as watching others, became my pseudo-mentor.

The genesis of this book is simply to remind myself, and tell others, what insights a mentor would have shared with me if he or she had the chance. These chapters are by no means industry or school specific, nor are they all-inclusive. The stories shared and the insights gained apply to all endeavors – personal, scholastic, and professional.

Not all of them will apply to you. Most of them you already know and may just need a simple reminder of. Over the years, I've found that most everyone I've shared these ideas with has substantial experience and more than a passing understanding of the concepts. However, because learning is lifelong and memory is sometimes short, the following pages are not only reminders to myself, but to you.

The term "outliers" came into the forefront of my vocabulary after reading Malcolm Gladwell's book: *Outliers: The Story of Success.* In it, he argues that success in any field requires practicing a specific task for at least 10,000 hours. He also discusses the different variables which contribute to a person achieving extreme success.

In an article in *USA Today*, Gladwell was quoted as saying, "The biggest misconception about success is that we do it solely on our smarts, ambition, hustle and hard work." I agree. Success – at least in the business, sports, and entertainment worlds – takes a myriad of activities, a measure of luck, and some God-given talent.

I'm not simply talking about the tangibles (I.Q., strength, speed, agility) and intangibles (birth order, where you were born, and what your parents taught you) that go into making someone successful. Although some measure of "success" will come from following the ideas shared in this book, demonstrable success measures only a fraction of the capacity each of us has to "alter our own stars" and rescript our own future.

My goal in writing this book is to remind students that outliers walk among us, and that anyone can become "markedly different in value [and value(s)] from the rest of the sample." In others words, you too can be less worried, more productive, more positive, and more secure. It's actually very easy – turn the page, and let's get on with it.

The Ego: Good or Bad?

The sound carries farther
when someone else blows your horn.
~ Harvey Mackay

Do you have an ego? Do I? Sure, we all do, and it's neither good nor bad. It simply means "self." The problem begins when it becomes the dominant factor in our lives. Then it's called egotism, defined as "the practice of talking about oneself too much," or "an exaggerated sense of self-importance." I often use a quote from the late, great football coach, Frank Leahy, of Notre Dame fame, who described egotism as "the anesthetic which dulls the pain of stupidity."

Of course, it's hard to develop "an exaggerated sense of self-importance" when the needle on your ego-meter typically points to somewhere south of mediocre – or worse! Growing up in the sixties and seventies, I played about every sport available to kids. You name it – football, basketball, boxing, baseball, etc. I was mediocre at them all. There was little to get egotistical about.

I didn't have much of a killer instinct, so my father used to smack me on the side of the head before boxing matches. He told me he was attempting to get me mad at my upcoming opponent. I remember very clearly telling him I was only getting mad at him.

Most of my athletic career was spent on one bench or another, collecting a variety of colored splinters and not getting to play until long after the game was decided. It wasn't that I didn't care – I really cared! It was simply that other than being tall, I possessed a minimum of God-given talent.

Somehow, I made the freshman "B" team in basketball, but didn't get a lot of playing time. So, during the summer between freshman and sophomore years, I made it my mission in life to become a basketball "phenom." To that end, I took at least a thousand shots a day, every day of the spring, summer, and early fall. By the end of that time, the one thing I could do was shoot.

Unfortunately at the time, but ultimately very fortunately, I was cut from the basketball team during the tryouts in sophomore year – more on that in a bit.

While quite bad at sports, I was worse in school. I used to pretend I was asleep when my parents returned from parent-teacher conferences. I suspect they had some indication of my grades when I'd be heading off to bed at six p.m. I really tried at sports, but didn't exert much effort at school. My high school grades never were higher than a very occasional B. Actually, I remember receiving more Ds than Bs. Ultimately, I think I graduated in the bottom quartile of my class.

Bad Examples

There's an old saying that "there's no such thing as a complete failure; you can always be used as a bad example." One guy who more than met that definition was a pilot I knew named Bobby, who had a hangar next to mine at Scottsdale (Arizona) Airport. Bobby had a massive ego about his flying skills, despite more than one case of failing to lower his landing gear, resulting in what's known as "gear-up" landings. Such landings, of course, cause significant damage to the plane, and certainly don't enhance the pilot's reputation for safety.

After the first crash, Bobby reportedly told the FAA investigators that his copilot was to blame for the failure to lower the landing gear and got off almost scot-free – except for the wrecked aircraft and momentarily damaged (yet still monumental) ego. Not long afterward, Bobby experienced his second gear-up landing – this time while piloting a rare, old and irreplaceable military plane. His only comment: "At least I stayed on the center line." He was referring to the center of the runway where his plane skidded and sparked to a complete stop, never to fly again.

Such incidents are remarkable for many reasons. When a plane's airspeed drops below a certain point, the gear warning horn automatically starts going off. It's so obnoxious and loud that it's impossible to mistake it for anything else, and should cause the pilot to lower the gear, if for no other reason than to stop the unbearable noise. It's the aviation equivalent to getting slapped upside the head.

Unfortunately, there are lots of folks like Bobby out there, in virtually every field of endeavor you can name. Their egos are so bloated that they don't hear the "gear warnings" going off. They'll do things their way, with little or no regard for common sense, sound judgment, and established procedures.

Over the years, I've seen many other examples of egotism in action, and the outcomes are invariably bad. To make matters worse, the egotist will not only fail to take responsibility for these negative outcomes, but, like Bobby, will often blame others for what happened. In the business world, being on the receiving end of this can be financially painful. In the medical world, it can cost a life.

It happens like this. One of our former emergency room attending physicians told a nurse who came to him concerned about the condition of a very ill child: "When you get your medical degree, come back and we'll chat about it." His egotism wouldn't allow him to accept advice from a "lowly" nurse.

In other circumstances, a junior resident or nurse or paramedic makes a statement to the attending physician about a patient: "Doctor, are you sure that patient is ready for discharge? She's still tachycardic (rapid heart rate)." The physician believes his authority or competence is threatened, and responds: "When you go to medical school and residency, maybe I'll listen to you. Now discharge the patient." The nurse obliges and the patient dies. Sadly, it happens. I can't tell you how many times nurses I work with save me from doing something stupid and the patient from a bad outcome.

Easy Prey

A physician friend told me a story about Bellevue Hospital in New York City. It was very early one morning. Until about 2 a.m., the emergency department was getting crushed with patients – suffering from overdoses to gunshot wounds and everything in between.

Suddenly, there was a lull in the onslaught and for the first time, the ED physicians, covered with blood, vomit and grime, were finally able to sit down for a moment's rest. Just as they did, the pneumatic doors opened and a man staggered in. One of the residents said: "Oh, Lord, help me, not another drunk!" Just then, the man fell flat on his face with an arrow sticking out of his back. The other resident stood up and yelled, "Circle the wagons!"

People with large egos are much like the poor guy impaled by the arrow. They have a large target on their back. It's easy to take advantage of someone whose ego prevents him or her from seeking assistance. Physicians, for example, are often seen as making poor business decisions. I suspect the root cause is that many of us think, "How hard can this be? I made it through medical school."

The Flip Side

Do these stories suggest that egotism is an unavoidable occupational hazard for doctors, as well as for other successful professionals and business leaders? Absolutely not! For every egotist I've met, I've known many men and women who consistently display the opposite character trait – humility.

It was the late author Frederick L. Collins who captured both the egotistical and the humble in these words: "Always remember there are two types of people in the world: those who come into a room and say, 'Well, here I am!' and those who come in and say, 'Ah, there you are.'" The choice is ours.

I once heard humility described as "as strange thing. The moment you think you've got it, you've lost it." The late author Helen Nielsen compared it to underwear: "essential, but indecent if it shows."

The Burger Salesman

Recently, a colleague of mine, a former bank president, told me of a lesson he'd unexpectedly learned many years ago. A stranger had come into the bank lobby and had approached one of the officers about cashing a check. He presented identification and, while his check was being approved and processed, the officer asked him what he did for a living.

The man said simply: "I sell hamburgers." That was certainly true but, in passing up the opportunity to impress that bank officer by mentioning how many hamburgers he sold every day, he made sure his "underwear" wasn't showing. After receiving his cash, he simply expressed his thanks and left.

When the president asked the officer the stranger's name, he showed him the check. The name on it, which the young officer hadn't recognized, was Ray Kroc. Twenty years earlier, the then 55-year old Kroc had launched what would become a nationwide – and later worldwide – chain of hamburger restaurants: McDonald's. By the time of that bank visit, Kroc was famous, and his company had sold hundreds of millions of hamburgers.

Kroc saw no need to inform that banker of his business empire or mention his achievements. His simple answer was characteristic of his humility. For example, whenever he was acclaimed as "an overnight success," he'd simply reply: "I was an overnight success all right, but thirty years is a long, long night." Ego trips were not on his itinerary.

Over the years, I've been very fortunate to be involved in a lot of really amazing things, and to meet some phenomenally gifted people. The one trait common to all of them has been a profound humility. Like Ray Kroc, they don't brag or overwhelm the conversation; they haven't gone on and on telling me about themselves or name dropping. They haven't needed to – they're simply and quietly confident. I'd like you to meet a few of them.

Somebody's Mom

I serve on the Board of Trustees for my alma mater, Drake University, where I graduated in 1982 with a degree in criminology and sociology. Drake wasn't always the highly regarded academic institution it is today. I was told when I applied that it was called the "Harvard of the Midwest."

Full disclosure: the year I was accepted (1978), Drake took in more than ninety percent of the applicants, the highest acceptance rate in its history. On seeing my high school grades, whoever was calling Drake the "Harvard of the Midwest" should have been dismayed. In fact, if I applied today, or during any other period of the school's history, I'd never get in.

As board members, we meet quarterly, acting as stewards and fiduciaries of the university. I enjoy it immensely. What I enjoy most is meeting with students. They're smart, motivated, articulate, and still have that "shiny new car" sheen. Board members often meet for lunch with various student groups and sit among the students who are, as a rule, not shy about sharing their thoughts about the university.

On one occasion, I was paired with a new board member and about five students. The areas the students were exploring and writing research papers about were unbelievable – cutting edge ideas just over the horizon. I learned a ton from them.

As this was all about the students, I shared little about myself, and the new board member I was seated next to shared nothing about her background. She asked a few questions but otherwise sat listening intently to the students with a warm smile on her face. In fact, I still only knew her first name, Marsha. If I had to describe her, it would be, "She's somebody's mom." I'm not even sure what I mean by that. She simply looked warm, engaging, nonjudgmental and friendly – someone's mom. But I was about to learn a lesson from her as well. It wasn't in anything she said; it was simply by her demeanor.

After lunch, we walked back to the meeting and I had the chance to do a bit of cyber-stalking on my phone. I looked at the board website and figured out her last name was Ternus. I still had no idea who she was until I Googled her name. Marsha Ternus was the former Chief Justice of the Iowa Supreme Court. In fact, she was the first female Chief Justice in the history of that court.

Little did I know, Marsha Ternus was a "rock star." Her presence in the Drake Community will be positively felt by the entire university for years to come. Yet, there she was quietly sitting among a group of students who were excitedly discussing their research, while she selflessly and humbly listened to their sometimes overly detailed (and over my head) explanations.

Speed of Sound

Terri was a vivacious marketing and public relations expert we employed at NextCare. She and her sister Tracy are twins and give new meaning to the word "identical." They finish each other's sentences, laugh before the punch lines of each other's jokes, and enjoy a sameness shared only by twins. Remarkably, they each married a fighter pilot – but, in talking with them, you'd never have guessed their occupation nor their achievements. There isn't a trace of ego in either man.

Terri's husband Aaron is an F-16 (Viper) pilot, whose last deployment was flying lead solo with the Air Force Thunderbirds. Aaron was simply the best of the best. He looked, acted and was every bit a walking recruitment poster for Air Force aviation.

One of Aaron's most endearing qualities is humility. Despite his accomplishments, his war record, and his rapid rise through the ranks of the Air Force, Aaron is as low key and as humble as anyone you'll ever meet. Although he has "rock star" status, this vignette is not about him.

It was through Aaron and Terri that I met Tracy's husband Matt, an Air Force Academy graduate who was also a Viper pilot. He was one of a select group of pilots chosen to first fly the F-35. Officially named the Lockheed Martin F-35 Lightning II, this single-seat, single-engine fifth generation fighter aircraft was designed for multiple roles, including ground attack, reconnaissance, and stealth missions. Matt is also at the top of the pyramid of a group of "A-gamers."

On one occasion, Matt and I planned to fly from Mesa, Arizona down to Tucson to watch Aaron perform in the first Thunderbird show of the season, presented for the Air Force personnel stationed at Davis-Monthan Air Force Base. We'd be flying in an old Korean War-era fighter trainer, a T-28 "B" Model, affectionately called "The Trojan," which I've owned and flown for the last twelve years.

After doing the preflight, we climbed up on the wing to start getting strapped in. Like most fighter pilots of today, Matt didn't have any "round engine prop-time." Despite his thousands of hours of jet time, his combat experience and obvious expertise, this was an entirely new experience for him.

He'd listened intently during the preflight, asking relevant questions, and was genuinely interested in the background and flying characteristics of a piece of aviation history. As he was strapping into the parachute, I began explaining the egress procedure, should we have to bail out. Mind you, I've never had to bail out of a plane and have never parachuted. In fact, the only time I'll ever bail out is if we're on fire. Otherwise, I'm flying it to the ground.

Bailing out of the T-28 is reported to be easy: blow off the canopy using a compressed nitrogen charge; unplug the communication cord attached to your helmet; roll the plane inverted; unbuckle your belt; and let Newton (a/k/a Gravity) take care of the rest.

As I was explaining the procedures in detail to Matt, it occurred to me that I wasn't sure if Air Force pilots, as part of their training, had to actually skydive (They don't. They're towed behind a vehicle until they get to about 500 feet, then are released and parachute to the ground so they can experience a landing).

As I was explaining how to pull the rip cord, I stopped and asked Matt if he'd ever jumped. He flashed a shy smile and remarked, "Well, if we jump today, it will be my 762nd time. I was part of the Air Force Academy demonstration sky dive team."

I replied, "Okay then, here's how we're going to do it. I'm going to watch you and do everything you do!"

What's so remarkable is that both Matt and Aaron have more to boast about than most of us. Yet, they don't spend one second trying to impress anyone, not even when given the obvious opportunity from a poser like me who was trying to explain how to jump out of an aircraft. The "real deals" don't need to boast; their actions and backgrounds speak for themselves.

Fragile – Handle with Care

Ego driven, insecure individuals can't bear to crack the thin veneer of their egos and thus won't venture into the unknown. In other words, they won't push the envelope. It's only when you do push the envelope that you discover your limits. Without raising the bar or pushing the envelope, you'll likely never fail at much and thus never get to really make lasting contributions.

Ultimately, and this is the take home point, the larger the ego, the more constrained and less successful the individual becomes. It's the ability to take risks, to have your ego bruised, to get up, dust yourself off and press on, which changes the world. Thus, what individuals with huge egos don't realize is that failure is a gift.

FOOD FOR THOUGHT

If I could pick only one area upon which to work it would be humility. Having a large ego or being "vainglorious" has so many negative repercussions that solving this issue alone will pay lifelong dividends. The short anwer: be the first to be able to laugh at yourself and don't take yourself too seriously.

IN OTHER WORDS

*When you are older you will know that
life is a long lesson in humility.*
~ J.M. Barrie

*Stay hungry, stay young, stay foolish,
stay curious, and above all, stay humble.*
~ Tom Hiddleston

Humility is so shy. If you begin talking about it, it leaves.
~ Timothy Keller

*As you grow up, always tell the truth, do no harm to others,
and don't think you are the most important being on earth.*
~ Harper Lee

*Humility is not thinking less of yourself;
it is thinking of yourself less.*
~ C.S. Lewis

If you want people to think well of you,
do not speak well of yourself.
~ Blaise Pascal

It's humbling to start fresh. It takes a lot of courage.
But it can be reinvigorating. You just have to
put your ego on a shelf and tell it to be quiet.
~ Jennifer Ritchie Payette

One of the greatest lessons is humility. Humility is
like oxygen to the soul. You won't get too far without it!
~ Dina Rolle

Humility is strong, not bold; quiet, not speechless;
sure, not arrogant.
~ Estelle Smith

Swallow your pride occasionally.
It's non-fattening.
~ Frank Tyger

CHAPTER

Failure: Nothing to Fear

It is impossible to live without failing at something,
unless you live so cautiously that
you might as well not have lived at all.
~ J. K. Rowling

When J.K. Rowling spoke those words, she wasn't simply expressing an opinion or a theory. Yes, the *Harry Potter* books have brought her enormous wealth and worldwide fame. The seven books in the series have sold about 450 million copies in more than 60 languages. She is, by virtually every measure, a "rock star," an outlier.

When she speaks about failure, it's with the voice of experience. She spoke those words I quoted above as the featured speaker for the 2008 commencement ceremonies at prestigious Harvard University. Yet, less than a dozen years earlier, that would have been incomprehensible. During the seven-year period between 1990 and 1997, Joanne Rowling had experienced the death of her mother and a divorce. She was a single mom, unemployed and existing on welfare. It was a difficult and depressing time in her life.

Despite the failures she'd experienced, one thing that kept her hopes alive was the novel she'd dreamed of writing, and had been working on for years. Somehow, she'd found a literary agent, but publisher after publisher rejected her manuscript. Finally, in 1997, one publisher offered her a small advance and agreed to print one thousand copies. The rest, of course, is history.

Now, I'm not suggesting that I've ever experienced trials and failures to the extent Joanne did before turning her dreams into reality, and becoming an outlier. But, as I think back on my teenage years, I had lots of setbacks – or failures – or flops, or whatever you choose to call them. And they seemed a lot more serious then than they do now.

For example, I didn't believe I had a tremendous amount going for me in basketball as I started my sophomore year in high school (or for that matter, during any of the previous years). I'm not sure I gave it a lot of thought; I simply knew I hadn't yet demonstrated that I excelled at much of anything.

As I mentioned in Chapter 1, I'd made the "B Team" during my freshman year basketball season, but spent most of the time on the bench. During previous summers, I'd attended both Ray Meyer's (famous DePaul University coach) and Dick Motta's (well regarded coach of the Chicago Bulls) basketball camps. Still, my high school coach told me I didn't have a "head for the ball." I think he missed the irony of his comment, in that every time I attempted to guard Shawn, our starting 6'8" center, he'd actually elbow me on *top* of my head. Time after time, his bony elbows would come crashing down on my skull like a flesh-covered hammer. I was pretty sure, given the lumps I took, that I must have a head for something!

Despite my repetitive head injuries, or maybe because of them, I was determined to make a better showing my sophomore year. To that end, I took a thousand shots per day, on my driveway, in our school's gym, or at the local park. I got to be such a good shot that one of my former basketball nemeses started saying "automatic" every time I took a shot.

As a result, I could shoot the pants off anyone, but the rest of my game was still below par. Despite being 6'1" as a sophomore (tall at the time), I couldn't touch the rim. I was slow on my feet and often fouled the person I was guarding – and even some players I wasn't! When I went out for the team my sophomore year, I thought, given the hours I'd spent in the gym and on my driveway, that I was a shoo-in.

As I recall, the tryouts lasted four days and people were cut at the end of each day. On the very last day, there were eighteen people left for twelve spots. The very last thing we did was line up at the free throw line. The head coach said whoever made two free throws in a row would automatically make the team. I suspect he thought that, given the pressure of the moment, everyone he didn't want on the team would probably not make them, giving him an excuse to cut them.

I was third in line. The two kids in front of me were both better players, yet they each made just one of the two shots, putting their basketball future at risk. I walked up to the free throw line cool as a cucumber. After all, I'd taken more than a hundred thousand shots over the preceding four months so, if anyone was ready for this moment, I was.

I took a deep breath, bounced the ball twice, stepped up, and swished the first shot. Everyone clapped. I stepped away from the line, took another deep breath, stepped up, dribbled twice, and made the second shot. Everyone cheered! I was on the team and felt like I'd just won the Nobel Prize. OK, I'm being dramatic; nonetheless, it felt really good.

I walked to the end of the line and cheered my teammates who made two in a row and consoled the ones who didn't. After everyone had gone, the results were tallied up; four of us had qualified. There were eight spots left to be chosen from the remaining fourteen kids. At the end of the drill, the coaches went off to confer while we all waited anxiously. Well, not all of us. The four of us who made the two shots were pretending to be nervous, but actually weren't.

A Broken Promise

After about five minutes, the coaches came back. The head coach thanked us for our hard work, gave a short speech about work ethic, and then read the names of the twelve players chosen. After every name was read, the lucky person was slapped on the back by those around him and congratulated. There were seven of us still standing there when it came time to read the final name. When the coach read it, I was shocked. It wasn't mine!

How could this be? I'd made two shots in a row. He'd made a promise and then broke it. I was furious, shocked, and sad, all at the same moment. After he dismissed us, I walked up to him and said, "Excuse me, Coach, but you said, if we made two in a row, we were on the team and I made two in a row." His only response: "Yes, you did."

And that was that. In the great grand scheme of things, it was merely a bump in the road. Looking back, it was a very poignant moment and maybe one of the best things that ever happened to me. The lessons that coach taught me, unintentionally, have been lifelong, and have helped me endure all sorts of failures and injustices, real and imagined.

In no particular order, here's what I learned:

1. Sometimes in life things aren't fair and there's simply nothing you can do about it, other than get over it and move on.

2. That how you respond to failure is usually more important than the reason you failed.

3. That not everyone plays by the rules. People go back on promises, lie, cheat and steal. So what! Rise above it and then move beyond.

4. Persevere and never, ever give up.

5. That hard work doesn't always mean success.

The Rest of the Story

I continued to practice and to take a lot of shots every day, and I made the team my junior and senior year. During the latter year, every senior on the team quit except Shawn (whose elbows were still razor sharp) and me. Yet, I was still sitting on the bench. By that time, I was 6'4", weighed 220 pounds, and was one of the bigger kids in the school. I could bench 315 pounds but was still slow and still couldn't jump.

However, my size caught the eye of the head football coach – the same guy who'd cut me from the basketball team two years earlier – and he asked me to play football for him. I told him I would have tried out but was afraid of getting cut by him – again. He got the message and walked away. It was a stupid, immature thing to say and, afterward, I regretted saying it. But, for those few seconds, I again felt like I'd won the Nobel Prize. No, I'm not being dramatic.

Other Sports

I wish I could tell you that, during my school years, I finally found where my talents lay, and that I went on to athletic stardom in another sport or two. Such, however, is not the case. As a high school freshman, I joined our track team – as a pole vaulter! My adventures on a basketball court had already revealed an inability to jump more than a few inches, so I figured that long pole would allow me to reach – uhh – new heights!

Sadly, when our high jumper, minus a pole, easily outjumped me, long pole and all, I knew it was time to look elsewhere. If altitude wasn't my thing, maybe distance would be, so I took up discus throwing. In fact, I got pretty good at it. As a senior, I was ranked among the better discus throwers in our area. But don't get too impressed; that's like saying I was the tallest midget.

My modest achievements in that sport gave me the courage to pursue it at the college level, and I tried out for the track and field team at Drake University. That lasted until a major competition, when I released my discus a tad early, propelling it into a crowd of runners competing in the 10,000-meter race. Nearly maiming several Somali runners proved to be perhaps the most noteworthy non-accomplishment in my athletic "career." To sum it up, as a student athlete, I'd failed. I was a flop!

Flopping: Not All Bad

With most things in life, there are usually both good and bad sides. Consider the case of one man who turned flopping into a new art form, achieving worldwide fame in the process. As a high schooler, he wanted to compete on the track team (sound familiar?). His goal was to be a high jumper, but he was unable to clear the bar at the required minimum of five feet.

He'd never been comfortable with the "straddle" style of jumping that had long been used by nearly everyone. After a running start, the jumper would propel his body upward, facing forward and toward the ground, then lifting each leg individually as it passed over the bar. It was a complex maneuver and so, at age 16, he began working on a new method. It called for him to turn his back to the bar, then leap upward, crossing head first with his body curved and then lifting his legs in the air.

He became so successful that, having once failed to clear five feet, he'd passed the six-foot mark by his junior year and was routinely jumping nearly six-and-a-half feet. His method was so unusual that, years before Facebook or Twitter or Yahoo, it still began to attract nationwide publicity. In 1964, one newspaper reporter described him as looking like "a fish flopping in a boat," as he crossed over the bar. Richard Douglas Fosbury was then 18 years old, two years removed from his failure to clear even five feet.

His method would quickly become known worldwide as the "Fosbury Flop," and Dick Fosbury would continue to move the bar higher and higher. In 1968, while competing for Oregon State University, he won both the NCAA championship and the U.S. Olympic Trials. In both events, and still a teenager, he jumped more than seven feet. Later that summer, he won a gold medal at The Olympic Games in Mexico City.

Dick Fosbury might easily have quit when, at age 16, he failed to clear even five feet as a high jumper. Instead, he used that failure as the starting point to not simply some personal success, but to a technique that would revolutionize his sport. For example, of all those who earned medals in the men's Olympic high jumping events held since 1972, the overwhelming majority used the "Fosbury Flop," and today, it continues to be the most popular high jumping technique.

Learning from Failure

I won't bore you with the details but, as my parents could testify, I didn't do any better as a student than I did as an athlete. The worst days for me were the ones when my report cards arrived. (Come to think of it, they weren't such great days for my parents either.) It wasn't until after I started college that I began getting my act together. While I've made some progress, I've still had perhaps more than my share of flops, and there are no guarantees they're all in the past. But I've worked hard to minimize them, and I can honestly say that in every flop, every failure, there is also a flip – a lesson I've taken from it. I've learned far more from them than I have from whatever modest success I've had.

I've one more story to tell you about another writer who overcame failure, a young man who'd fallen so far that he thought suicide might be his only answer. His name was Augustine and, from early childhood, his mother had instilled in him the desire to become a writer when he grew up. Together, they dreamed that dream. In high school, he edited the school newspaper and, after graduation, planned to attend the highly rated School of Journalism at the University of Missouri.

Then, when he was 17, a heart attack took his mom's life, and he was devastated. The dream, he thought, was over. It was 1940 and World War II had just begun, so instead of heading to college, he enlisted in the U.S. Army Air Corps (now the U.S. Air Force). Trained as a bombardier, he flew 30 combat missions over Germany during that war.

After the war ended, he returned home and married his childhood sweetheart. A year later, the couple became parents of a baby girl. But there were problems. Lacking a college education, Augustine had trouble finding a job that would support his family. He tried selling life insurance but it was hard, and he'd stop off on his way home "for one drink" at a local bar.

His drinking became so severe that his wife left him, taking along their daughter. Then he lost both his house and his job. Years later, he would say, "I was a drunk, a 35-year-old bum, ready to end it all. I had thirty dollars in my pocket, and when I saw a gun in a pawnshop for twenty-nine dollars, I almost bought it."

Instead, somehow, he found himself at a local library, where he picked up a motivational book and began to read. Soon, he was visiting other libraries, reading every motivational book he could find. He contacted the author of one of them, who offered him a job as a salesman. Before long, he was promoted to sales manager, at least partly as a result of a sales manual he'd written for his company.

Writing that manual also rekindled the spark that had nearly been extinguished when his mother died. From sales manager, he was named editor of the company's motivational magazine. Finding the name Augustine too formal, he began to abbreviate it in his columns as simply Aug, and later changed the spelling to Og.

Beginning with his book, *The Greatest Salesman in the World*, Og Mandino would write more than a dozen inspirational and motivational books, and become the most famous and successful inspirational writer in the world. His books have sold more than fifty million copies in some two dozen languages. He was also a popular speaker, and was inducted into the Hall of Fame of the National Speakers Association.

Og Mandino, who died in 1996, is still widely read and quoted. Many of his quotes are among my favorites, but perhaps the following one best sums up the message of this chapter: "Remind thyself, in the darkest moments, that every failure is only a step toward success."

─── FOOD FOR THOUGHT ───

As momentarily painful as failure can be, looking back, my own failures have opened up doors and led me to some of the best times and biggest successes of my life.

─── IN OTHER WORDS ───

Most of us handle failure in one of several ways.
We blame it on somebody else, we deny it happened, we become embarrassed by it or we totally lose confidence and give up.
You have a fifth avenue and that's to rise from your ashes.
~ Dale Brown

Failure is an event, never a person.
~ William D. Brown

You build on failure. You use it as a stepping stone.
Close the door on the past. You don't try to forget the mistakes,
but you don't dwell on it. You don't let it have any of your
energy, or any of your time, or any of your space.
~ Johnny Cash

Failure isn't the end of the world—
it's just the end of that experiment.
~ Holley Gerth

Failure doesn't consist in stumbling and falling. The failure is
staying there on the floor. Success is finding something while
you're down there to pick up with you.
~ James S. Hewett

Failures are like skinned knees,
painful but superficial.
~ H. Ross Perot

*I've missed over 9,000 shots in my career.
I've lost almost 300 games. 26 times I've been trusted to take
the game-winning shot...and missed. I've failed over and over
and over again in my life. And that is why I succeed.*

~ Michael Jordan

*My great concern is not whether you have failed,
but whether you are content with your failure.*

~ Abraham Lincoln

*It's when you run away
that you're most liable to stumble.*

~ Casey Robinson

*Failure should be our teacher, not our undertaker.
Failure is delay, not defeat. It is a temporary detour,
not a dead-end street.*

~ William Arthur Ward

*You can be discouraged by failure—or you can learn from it.
So go ahead and make mistakes. Make all you can.
Because, remember that's where you'll find success.
On the far side.*

~ Thomas J. Watson

Make failure your teacher, not your undertaker.

~ Zig Ziglar

Press On!

If you're trying to achieve, there will be roadblocks.
I've had them; everybody has had them. But obstacles don't have to
stop you. If you run into a wall, don't turn around and give up.
Figure out how to climb it, go through it, or work around it.
~ Michael Jordan

Michael Jordan, perhaps the greatest and most successful basketball player of all time, was right on. Obstacles! Roadblocks! Everybody has had them, but no matter how big they may seem to you, they don't have to stop you. In fact, if you change your perspective, they'll energize you!

For example, suppose you'd been dreaming since childhood of becoming a TV journalist when you grew up. That seems reasonable enough, even though you're being raised by a single mom in a poor Baltimore neighborhood and dreaming of a career in which there had been relatively few African-Americans. Such circumstances may sound like *reasons* but they're really just *excuses*, and I once heard an excuse defined as: "the skin of a reason, stuffed with lies."

Excuses aside, there is at least one huge obstacle in your path, you stutter! Badly! At age 12, you're declared to be "functionally illiterate." You're subjected to so much ridicule by your public school classmates that your mother moves you to a private school, something she can ill afford.

But we can stop supposing, because that's exactly what happened to a boy named Byron Pitts. Until shortly before he was due to enter high school, he still couldn't read – another major roadblock to a television career. But he didn't quit; for one thing, his mother wouldn't hear of it. He would later write: "She'd tell me, 'Keep your head up, no matter what.'" Every night, with her help, he spent hours reading and studying. He progressed to the point where he became a sports reporter for his high school newspaper.

In his 2009 biography, *Step Out on Nothing: How Faith and Family Helped Me Conquer Life's Challenges*, Pitts wrote: "I loved sports, and I was beginning to love words," he says. "There was something so rewarding about watching people read an article I had written. It would make me think back to the days when people thought I was stupid. Now people were reading my words in the paper."

After graduating from high school, he enrolled in Ohio Wesleyan University, majoring in Journalism and Speech Communication. Encouraged by the obstacles he'd overcome, he set an even higher career goal. No longer would he settle on simply becoming a TV journalist. His new dream was to become a correspondent on the long-running and prestigious CBS news magazine: *60 Minutes*.

But there were still roadblocks in his path. In his university classes, his late start as a reader continued to challenge him. At one point, he was placed on academic probation after receiving a "D" grade in an English class. He repeated the class in the following semester and, to his dismay, received only a "D+."

Calling him aside, his professor said: "Mr. Pitts, your presence at Ohio Wesleyan University is a waste of my time and the government's money. I think you should leave."

Of that moment, Pitts writes: "I was eighteen years old, and this man, this teacher, crushed my dreams." Fortunately, another English professor happened upon him as he sat weeping. Because of her encouragement and guidance, he went on to earn his degree and embark on a career that would see him not only reach his goals but become a winner of multiple awards at both the national and regional levels.

Pitts began his career as an intern at a local TV station in Durham, North Carolina and moved on to stints as a reporter and weekend anchor at various stations along the East Coast. He joined CBS in 1997, based as a news correspondent in Miami and then Atlanta, before his 2001 transfer to CBS headquarters in New York. His coverage of the World Center terrorist attacks in New York earned him his first national Emmy Award.

He continued to cover major new stories around the world, including the fall of Saddam Hussein in Iraq in 2003, Hurricane Katrina in New Orleans in 2005, and the major earthquake in Haiti in 2010. His work not only brought more awards but he became chief national correspondent for CBS News before landing his dream job as a member of the *60 Minutes* team. The "functionally illiterate" teenager who was told he was wasting his time in college had come a long way, refusing to allow the obstacles in his path to keep him from achieving his dreams.

In 2006, Byron Pitts returned to Ohio Wesleyan University as the commencement speaker, using the occasion to pay tribute to Dr. Ülle Lewes, the English professor who, twenty-four years earlier, had helped him overcome that final obstacle in his path. Asking her to stand, he said: "That day you didn't simply soothe my tears. You saved my life. Thank you for believing in me when I didn't believe in myself. Thank you for being my angel."

Then, turning to the graduates, he encouraged them: "Live each day as if it's your last. Don't simply be good—be better. Better isn't good enough, so be the best. Don't settle for your best. Be an angel."

Too Dumb to Quit?

After reading some of my elementary and high school report cards, my parents could not have been blamed had the words "functional illiterate" popped into their minds regarding their underachieving son. I certainly don't mean to imply that the obstacles I faced during my school years even remotely compared to those of Byron Pitts. And I readily concede that those I did face were entirely of my own making.

While I eventually got the message and cleaned up my act as a learner, I've encountered a variety of obstacles during my journey through life and, as Michael Jordan advised, have done my best to climb them, go though them, or work around them. For example, in 1993, I started a company called NextCare – on a shoestring. I literally worked day and night to get it up and running. During its early stage, one man backed out and another one said he didn't want to take on any more risk.

I pressed on and we were actually making headway when the bank called our loan and put us in the "workout" division. At the time, I thought this was great, because I liked to work out. Then I learned that this actually was the area of the bank where bad loans were handled. The bank could have called the note at any time, which meant it would have taken over and seized all our assets.

So we triple mortgaged our house and finally switched banks. When I went back and asked why the man who was our "workout banker" didn't simply demand payment, he told me it was because he never heard "defeat in my voice." I served as chairman and CEO of NextCare until 2010, by which time it had grown from a single clinic to fifty-eight clinics in six states, with annualized revenue of nearly one hundred million dollars.

Now maybe I'm just too dumb to quit, but remember: You're never beaten till you quit. For those who get into fights, the worst people to fight with are those who are too dumb to quit, because they just keep coming back.

A Shining Example

America's history is filled with stories of men and women whose "press on" and "never quit" attitudes are shining examples of the persistence and the persevering spirit on which our nation was built. Among my favorites is Theodore Roosevelt, the President of the United States from 1901 to 1909.

One of the most colorful and popular men to have ever served in that capacity, Roosevelt was far more than a political figure. He was, among other things, an adventurer, an historian, a hunter, a naturalist, an orator, an explorer, and an author. His prodigious literary output includes twenty-six books, more than a thousand magazine articles, and thousands of speeches and letters.

There are lots of examples of Roosevelt's persistence. In 1912, as he was about to begin a speech, he was shot in the chest by a would-be assassin. Undeterred, he proceeded to deliver his speech, after commenting to his audience: "Ladies and gentlemen, I don't know if you fully understand but I have just been shot, but it takes more than that to kill a Bull Moose." With blood seeping through his clothing, he then spoke for ninety minutes, before being taken to a hospital. The bullet would remain in his chest for the rest of his life.

In 1913, disappointed by a rare political defeat, Roosevelt wanted to get away from Washington, and accepted an invitation to speak in Argentina. While in South America, he joined forces with some Brazilian explorers to navigate a thousand-mile long tributary of the Amazon River, named the Rio da Duvida, the River of Doubt. It was a dangerous journey, one which nearly killed Roosevelt. Nevertheless, the team overcame one obstacle after another, successfully mapping the entire length of that river. In recognition of that amazing feat and of the courage and tenacity of its leader, Brazilian officials changed the river's name to Rio Roosevelt.

The story of that journey was told by author Candice Millard in her 2005 book, *The River of Doubt*. In the prologue, this is how she described

Roosevelt: "Each time he encountered an obstacle, he responded with more vigor, more energy, more raw determination. Each time he faced personal tragedy or weakness, he found his strength not in the sympathy of others, but in the harsh ordeal of unfamiliar new challenges and harsh adventure."

Theodore Roosevelt might well have been describing himself when he wrote these words:

> *"It is not the critic who counts, not the one who points out how the strong man stumbled or how the doer of deeds might have done better. The credit belongs to the man who is actually in the arena, whose face is marred with sweat and dust and blood; who strives valiantly; who errs and comes short again and again; who knows the great enthusiasms, the great devotions, and spends himself in a worthy cause; who, if he wins, knows the triumph of high achievement; and who, if he fails, at least fails while daring greatly, so that his place shall never be with those cold and timid souls who know neither victory nor defeat."*

The Fruits of Victory

Persistence, of course, is essential to achievement in any and all of life's endeavors, including sports. Perhaps the most eloquent expression of this truth I've ever heard came from the late General Douglas MacArthur, during the time he served as Superintendent of the United States Military Academy at West Point, New York. First uttered more than seventy years ago, his words stand at the entrance to Michie Stadium on the West Point campus, where the Army team has played football since 1924. These are his words: "Upon the fields of friendly strife are sown the seeds that, upon other fields, on other days, will bear the fruits of victory."

Included, of course, would be the seeds of persistence, or perseverance, whether it be in football or in any other sports. In my view, it may be most apparent in long-distance running. For example, the marathon, at 26 miles plus 385 yards, has become perhaps the ultimate test of a runner's stamina and perseverance, not only for professional athletes, but for the thousands of ordinary folks who enter – and complete – them.

But even marathons pale by comparison to other long-distance running achievements. For example, in recent years many men and women have run completely across the United States, a distance of more than 3,000 miles. That's an amazing feat of perseverance, but I recently read of an even more amazing one. In February 2012, an Australian named Pat Farmer completed a 13,000-mile run, starting at the North Pole and ending at the South Pole. It took him ten months, running an average of nearly two full marathons – every day – across 14 countries, to do so.

An Unlikely Hero

But my favorite long-distance running story is about another Australian, a man named Cliff Young, who didn't set any distance records, but nevertheless became a legend in his homeland.

It began in 1983, as the inaugural foot race from Sydney to Melbourne was about to get underway. It was an ambitious undertaking, covering a distance of 875 kilometers, or more than 540 miles. That's the equivalent of running nearly 21 complete marathons—in a row! To put it in perspective, it would be similar to running from New York City to Raleigh, North Carolina or from Los Angeles to Reno.

About one hundred and fifty superbly conditioned athletes had signed up to participate in what was expected to be a six-day event. So race officials were taken aback when Cliff Young showed up and requested an entry form, saying he was ready to go. This sixty-one year old sheepherder, wearing overalls and galoshes over his work boots, didn't exactly fit the picture of a world-class distance runner.

Convinced the man was either crazy or that it was some sort of publicity stunt, officials told him he couldn't run. But Cliff Young was determined to compete. He'd spent his life on his family's sprawling 2,000-acre farm, with 2,000 head of sheep. His was a poor family, he explained, and could afford neither horses nor tractors. Whenever the storms rolled in, Cliff's job was to start running and round up the sheep. It was no small task. Sometimes, he said it would take two or three days of running to finish the job.

It sounded like a totally improbable tale but, reluctantly, the officials allowed him to enter, hoping he wouldn't drop dead during the race. Off they went, and the world-class athletes were quickly out of sight, leaving old Cliff way behind, shuffling along in his galoshes. But no one had thought to explain to him that the race plan called for eighteen hours of running, followed by six hours of rest, so he just kept right on shuffling along. After all, it took perseverance to round up all those sheep when the storms came; there was never time to take even a short break.

By the fifth day, Cliff had caught and passed them all, easily winning the race, and becoming a national hero. It was the centuries-old Aesop's Fable, *The Hare and the Tortoise*, suddenly brought to life. Ironically, many of these super athletes who had first sneered at Cliff's peculiar shuffling style later adopted it themselves, finding it better suited for extremely long distances.

But there's more to this Cliff Young story – a lot more. For years, he continued to complete in ultra marathon events, training for them by running thirty kilometers (18.6 miles) a day on his farm. Then, at age seventy-six, he announced that he would try and become the oldest man to run completely around Australia, which is roughly the size of the continental United States.

The distance: 16,000 kilometers, or nearly 10,000 miles! It was an extraordinarily ambitious undertaking but, unfortunately, through no fault of his own, he was unable to achieve his goal. During the run, his only permanent crew member, who drove the support vehicle and provided Cliff with food and water, became ill, and he had to stop.

Cliff was very disappointed about having to quit the run after *only* 6,520 kilometers, or more than 4,000 miles. He'd been running for nearly three months, averaging the equivalent of about one-and-a-half marathons a day—at age seventy-six!

But it was more than his amazing feats of perseverance and courage that made Cliff Young a great man. He was an inspiration to millions and a great encourager of younger runners. In his honor and memory, in 2004, the year after his death at age 81, the organizers of the race where he first gained fame permanently changed its name to the Cliff Young Australian Six Day Race.

There are two other parts to the Cliff Young story. When he entered that first race in 1983, it never occurred to him that there was any prize money involved, and so he was quite surprised to learn he had won $10,000, a huge sum for that poor farmer. However, instead of keeping it, he gave $2,000 to each of the five runners who had finished most closely behind him.

And the main reason he was so disappointed at having to quit his run around Australia was that he had undertaken it in the first place to raise money for homeless children!

—————————— **FOOD FOR THOUGHT** ——————————

Give me people like Byron Pitts, Theodore Roosevelt, and Cliff Young – who won't quit, who have great attitudes, and who refuse to let obstacles or setbacks cause them to abandon their dreams. I'll hire them in a second. They will change the world and they *will be* very successful.

Here's the bottom line: If it was easy, everyone would do it. With ordinary talent and extraordinary perseverance, all things are attainable.

It's your choice. You can live in the world of regrets, the world of "If only...," of "I coulda, shoulda, woulda..." or you can follow the examples of those whose stories we've shared.

Perseverance, determination, tenacity, persistence—or whatever term you choose to describe it—is among the seeds that "on other fields, on other days, will bear the fruits of victory, which separate the achievers from the wishful thinkers. Don't let regrets replace your dreams. Follow this advice from the pen of Langston Hughes, the famous African-American poet and author: "Hold fast to dreams / For if dreams die / Life is a broken-winged bird / That cannot fly."

IN OTHER WORDS

Never quit, It is the easiest cop-out in the world. Set a goal and don't quit until you attain it. When you do attain it, set another goal, and don't quit until you reach it. Never quit."

~ Paul "Bear" Bryant

I do not know the word 'quit.' Either I never did, or I have abolished it.

~ Susan Butcher

If I had to select one quality, one personal characteristic that I regard as being most highly correlated with success, whatever the field, I would pick the trait of persistence. Determination. The will to endure to the end, to get knocked down seventy times and get up off the floor saying, 'Here comes number seventy-one!'

~ Richard M. DeVos

Persistent people begin their success where others end in failure.

~ Edward Eggleston

That which we persist in doing becomes easier –
not that the nature of the task has changed,
but our ability to do it has increased.
~ Ralph Waldo Emerson

The opportunity of a lifetime is to pick yourself.
Quit waiting to get picked; quit waiting for someone to
give you permission; quit waiting for someone to say you are
officially qualified and pick yourself.
~ Seth Godin

Progress is made by those who see a thing through
after the quitters have dropped out.
~ Richard C. Halverson

So long as there is breath in me, that long will I persist.
For now I know one of the greatest principles of success:
if I persist long enough I will win.
~ Og Mandino

Achievement is not always success, while reputed failure
often is. It is honest endeavor, persistent effort to
do the best possible under any and all circumstances.
~ Orison Swett Marden

The most essential factor is persistence – the determination
never to allow your energy or enthusiasm to be dampened by
the discouragement that must inevitably come.
~ James Whitcomb Riley

The whole idea is not to beat the other runners.
Eventually you learn that the competition is against the little
voice inside you that wants you to quit.
~ George Sheehan

*I just keep on doing what everyone starts out doing.
The real question is, why did other people stop?*
~ William Stafford

*Impossibilities crumble in the crucible of persistence;
difficulties disappear under the power of persistence.*
~ William A. Ward

CHAPTER

Communication and [Ya' Know] Stuff

The single biggest problem in communication
is the illusion that it has taken place.
~ George Bernard Shaw

It's been more than sixty years since the great Irish playwright I quoted above left this world but, if he were to return today, he'd be astonished at how much worse most attempts at communication have become since he labeled it as merely an "illusion." Back in his day, there were no computers, email, social media, or smart phones – just to name a few of today's tools which theoretically were meant to improve communication. He certainly could never have imagined that the primary body part needed for one party to convey information to another would be the thumb.

The word "texting" was unknown and that dreadful "Ya' know" had not yet become the phrase of choice of both the literary challenged and the glitterati. For example, professional actress and television personality Whoopi Goldberg, when she was a guest on the Fox New program *Hannity,* used the expression numerous times.

Well-educated Caroline Kennedy, daughter of the late JFK, used it many times a few years ago in attempting to explain why, ya' know, she thought she should, ya' know, be given Hillary Clinton's seat in the U.S. Senate. The ridicule heaped on her as a result may have had something to do with why, ya' know, she eventually withdrew.

What It's Not!

Let's start by spelling out what communication is *not*! Sending a letter, or an email, fax, text message, instagram, or tweet, etc. doesn't complete the process of communication. It's simply one step in the process – conveying information, or making an announcement.

The late Mortimer Adler, a popular American author and educator, described that process well. "Communication," he said, "is like playing catch. Catching is as much of a skill as throwing, though it is a skill of a different kind." Unfortunately, instead of catching what's been thrown and returning it, we seem to keep dropping the ball, and we've been doing so for a long time. To keep the "game" going properly requires transmission, reception, reaction, and response.

As the old saying goes: "It takes two to tango," which applies just as well to communication as it does to dancing. Two words which are used basically to cut off any attempt to connect – or communicate – are "whatever" and "stuff." Neither word leaves room for the dance to continue.

Whenever I hear the latter, it brings back memories of one of my favorite movie scenes. The film was titled *The Sure Thing*, in which one of the main characters, named Gib, was discussing with a friend his chances of getting a date with a very attractive classmate. The conversation went like this:

> **Gib's friend:** Forget her; I hear she only likes intellectuals.

> **Gib:** So? I'm intellectual and stuff.

> **Gib's friend:** You're flunking English. That's your mother tongue, and stuff.

The Conversation Dance

Speaking of conversation, that once popular means of communication is rapidly becoming an endangered species, but there's at least one man who's been working diligently to preserve it. A Las Vegas-based speaker and consultant, Loren Ekroth publishes a weekly ezine titled *The Better Conversations Newsletter.*

Also known as "Dr. Conversation," he's the founder of National Better Conversation Week, held each year in November. Loren says conversation "is like a dance. You must know the steps and you must dance in step with your partner."

Sadly, not a lot of dancing is going on these days. Everywhere you look, especially among young people, heads are down, buried in laptops, iPads, iPods and iPhones, thumbs twitching madly.

Older than I Realized

It's all Neil Papworth's fault. It was back on December 3, 1992 when this young British engineer sent a text message from his office computer to his boss's cell phone. The boss was at a Christmas party, and Papworth's message simply read "Merry Christmas." It was the first such message ever sent. [Aside to readers: typing that date took my breath away. For us "older folks," texting is a rather new phenomenon, so it startled me to realize it's been around all your lives.]

Papworth had no idea what he'd started. Years later, he told an interviewer he was still baffled by its popularity. He wondered where people found the time to text. He said he was averaging about ten to fifteen texts a week, and expressed regret over just one he'd been unable to send. It would have been to the young woman he later married. "I wanted to propose to her," he said, "but I realized she didn't have a phone." That would be a drawback.

Mixed Messages

In a relatively short time, text messaging has exploded as a means of sending and receiving information. Many of these messages serve a useful and important function; many others do not. Hundreds of thousands of texts are sent out every day. It's not my purpose here to become a prophet of doom, but I think we all recognize that text messaging has brought both its risks and rewards.

The statistics are breathtaking, and ignoring them would be reckless and irresponsible. Texting while driving causes more than one-and-a-half *million* accidents and upwards of three hundred thousand injuries every year, and is responsible for eleven teenage deaths *every day*. That's why I strongly applaud the current "Take the Pledge" campaign sweeping the country. The pledge simply states; "No text is worth the risk. It can wait." You can find out more about it at www.itcanwait. com.

Despite the dangers, text messaging can, and does, have a positive role to play in the communication process. According to one psychologist, "Texting can be an enormous tool. It offers companionship and the promise of connectedness."

A New Language

One outcome of the texting craze that neither Papworth nor anyone else could have foreseen would be the emergence of a brand new language, not one to be spoken but to be transmitted solely via thumb. By several estimates, it consists of some fourteen hundred abbreviations and acronyms, most of them undecipherable by those not familiar with the practice.

If you're part of that latter group (which includes me), you might enjoy visiting a website or two that list them. I predict you'll find them, in turn, clever, amusing, hilarious, crude, and utterly baffling.

The Tats Craze

Although the practice of permanently decorating the skin dates back centuries – even millennia – tattooing has recently undergone a revival to a degree perhaps never reached before. I'm not really sure what the point is, but I suspect that, at least in most cases, it's intended to send a message – of some sort. Why else would one allow various body parts to be pricked and punctured and then injected with various hues of ink? The purpose certainly can't be simply to stand and admire oneself in the bathroom mirror. Can it? The call to "read my lips" seems to have given way to "read my body."

I realize I'm seen in some circles as nearly prehistoric – I'll settle for middle-aged – but I'm puzzled by this "tat trend." Am I missing the point (pun intended)? The message – whatever it is – isn't coming through. And it's certainly a shortsighted practice. Decorated arms, legs, and other body parts may look good on a teenaged or twenty-something body, but the message or picture won't wear well over the long haul, especially when the grandma or grandpa stage arrives. The wrinkles are bound to distort the image originally intended.

Take a recent young patient of mine. For reasons I cannot fathom, he had the base of his rather small appendage tattooed with the symbol of the Nazi party. I can only imagine (and don't want to) what the symbol morphed into just prior to waking up in the morning or who the "artist" was who designed it. Does this mean I'm against the practice? Not necessarily, except that as a physician and a parent, I have some reservations. Other than that, my answer would be "whatever – ya know!"

OOPS!

One word of caution before I leave this subject: if the tat you're planning includes words, be sure to hire a good editor, or at least a proofreader. For example, a few years ago, a national magazine carried a brief item about a star player on one prominent university's football team. This young man wanted to honor his mother by having her first name – MABEL – emblazoned in four-inch high letters on his manly chest. And so the deed was done. Sadly, however, he had spelled dear old Mom's name as MABLE.

One final humorous tattoo, I recently saw "I'm Awsome" tattooed on an upper back. I wanted to write below: "except at spelling."

I must admit I'm not always the best or most appropriate in terms of my style or manner of communication. I've also learned over the years to take most things with a grain of salt (particularly if it's followed by a shot of tequila and a slice of lime), so I don't get too worked up over much of anything that's directed my way.

That said, I've learned a thing or two about how not to communicate and what not to say or write, mostly from experience. The following are styles of communication I frequently observe, which ultimately do little to further the intended discourse or outcome.

Non-verbal Communication

Renate Mousseux is a well-known and respected authority on body language, and has testified as an expert witness in numerous high-profile court cases. She has also been called on to interpret for television audiences the non-verbal signals of participants in such events as the three presidential debates between Barack Obama and Mitt Romney and Britain's most recent Royal Wedding.

In her seminars, titled *Body Language and Its Power*, she defines communication as "the transfer of information and ideas during interactions between people." She tells her audiences: "Considering the researched fact that we judge a person in less than four minutes, and that sixty-five percent of perceived messages are non-verbal, obviously Body Language plays an extremely important role both in daily business and private life."

Certainly, body language can send both positive and negative signals. In the latter category, here are a few common ones I've noted:

- Talking with your arms folded across your chest or with your fists clenched at your side. (It conveys aggressiveness.)

- Blowing your nose or wiping your mouth and then shaking someone's hand. (I'm not sure what it conveys but it's disgusting.)

- Rolling your eyes when someone is speaking to you. (My children will tell you this is a sure way for me to say: "The last thing I want to do is hurt you, but it's still on the list.")

- Talking over your shoulder while walking away or out of a room. (It conveys disrespect.)

- Crossing your legs and folding your arms while sitting. (It conveys that you're hiding something, or that you're cold.)

- Snapping gum or chewing with your mouth open. (It conveys that your parents were first cousins.)

- Shifting eyes or shifting your body back and forth while standing. (It conveys that you're being deceitful, or have to hit the bathroom!)

- Staring at the opposite sex in an inappropriate manner while talking to them. (Enough said. You know what I mean!)

- Working, reading, texting, writing or watching TV while someone is trying to have a conversation with you. I'm guilty of this one (it conveys disrespect) and I'm still working on always being "present" in the moment.

- Not making eye contact while speaking directly to others or shaking their hand while not looking at them. (It conveys lack of confidence.)

One important item about body language that Ms. Mousseux would add is this: "Never point at people, only at things."

Written Communication

There's no question that we're turning into a nation of functional illiterates. About the worst advice I've seen to remedy that problem in your writing is to rely on spellcheck programs. A couple of years ago, a popular magazine published an article titled *How to Appear More Intelligent,* and included this bit of really bad advice: "Spell-check. Seriously. This is one of the world's great inventions—maybe better than the wheel. Use it religiously to correct your typing mistakes."

Great invention? Better than the wheel? Not even close! Sure, a spellcheck program will catch some typing mistakes, but it will miss many others, and its grammatical suggestions are generally wrong as well.

Some years ago, an anonymous writer composed a fourteen-line poem titled *Check It Out*, and deliberately included numerous errors. The last time I counted, there were more than eighty of them. For example, here's the first of the seven two-line stanzas:

> "Eye halve a Spelling Checker, eye got four my,
> pea sea. It plane lee marques four my revue,
> miss steaks aye can knot sea."

Care to guess how many mistakes this "great invention" caught? If you said "None," you get a gold star. If you doubt it, I invite you to try it on your computer.

Here's my personal list of what to avoid in your writing:

- Frequently misspelling words or writing in different tenses.

- Spelling someone's name incorrectly, despite it being part of the correct email address. (This one always amazes me: "Dear Mr. Schoefelt," sent to jshufeldt@ingredientsofoutliers.com.)

- Using excessive legalese in a document (heretofore, etc.).

- Using email or written communication to convey important information that should be communicated in person. (For example, telling a close friend or long-time business partner, via email or voice mail, that you'll be dissolving the relationship!)

- CAPITALIZING EVERY WORD IN AN EMAIL OR TEXT MESSAGE.

- Using multiple exclamation points. (I was sooooo drunk last night!!!!!!!!)

- Using shortened versions of words or phrases in a business email. (Examples: prolly, ur, OMG, IDK, lol, eieio.)

- Multiple smiley faces, frowns, or any other kind of word art in a business email.

- Creatively interchanging: to, too and two; your and you're; its and it's; and their, they're and there.

- Excessively long sentences without any punctuation really drive me crazy almost more so than anything else even chewing gum with an open mouth or swearing in a meeting or one time at band camp this guy like really thought he was cool and then started drinking OMG he was so drunk that his parents were called and then he like he passed out in front of me.

- Using "I" and "me" interchangeably. ("Him and me went to the tractor pull and drank Buds.")

Verbal Communication

If there's one advantage this method has over written communication is that some of your mistakes won't be noticed. That's especially true of homonyms, words that sound alike but have different meanings (waiver and waver, vial and vile, etc.). In writing, of course, they jump right off the page.

I have dozens of illustrations to prove my point, but I'll leave you with just one which, as a physician, really caught my eye. It was a magazine article in which the author described a hospital visit where a lab technician took "vile after vile of blood." What was especially vile was this bit of writing.

Here are a few of the no-no's that get my attention:

- Saying "like" like every few words (I, for one, don't like it.)

- Using threats, "If you don't do XXX, then I'll do YYY!" (The conversation can only go one direction from here. It's rarely positive, as you leave the recipient no way out.)

- Speaking in the third person (although this is really fun; saying "John's getting angry!" is like super annoying).

- Mumbling, low-talking, or talking into the hand (sadly, I used to silently mouth words to my grandmother to see if I could make her tap her hearing aid. I'm sick, I know).

- When someone asks a legitimate question, respond by exclaiming, "I can't believe you didn't know that!" Or "Everybody knows that." (Conveys that you believe the person's that stupid.)

- Saying "Trust me," and then proceeding to say something completely untrue.

- Saying "I'll be honest with you," or "To tell you the truth," suggesting everything else you've said up to that point was a pack of lies.

- Starting sentences with the word, "Again." "Again, let me tell you what I think you obviously need to hear but clearly don't want to."

- Trailing off in midsentence and waiting for someone else to finish your sentence. "In 1930, the Republican controlled House of Representatives, in an effort to alleviate the effects of the… anyone, anyone, Great Depression, passed the… anyone, anyone, tariff bill, the Smoot-Hawley Tariff Act, which … anyone, anyone, raised or lowered… anyone, anyone, Buehler?"

- Interrupting while the other person hadn't stopped speaking.

Dropping the Ball

So far, most of this chapter has dealt with just one part of the communication process. The reason for what George Bernard Shaw called "the illusion that it has taken place" is because most of what's defined as communication is really one-directional activity, with no awareness of what's missing.

The individual who's speaking or writing isn't communicating until and unless there's a recipient to whom he or she is speaking or writing, and until that recipient acknowledges receiving it, and responds accordingly. The missing link in the communication process is the listener.

Often, what's taking place isn't communication, but dueling monologues. Even the casual bystander can plainly see that the one whose lips aren't moving isn't listening at all, but is simply waiting for the speaker to take a breath before pouncing.

Over the years, that sorry fact has been noted again and again. In 1982, newspaper columnist Jim Sanderson called listening: "one of the great lost arts in human relationships. People instinctively react to any opening you give them to talk about themselves." A few years later (1988), well-known author and speaker Leo Buscaglia commented: "It seems that few people listen anymore. . . I'm beginning to wonder if they [listeners] are a vanishing breed."

——————————— FOOD FOR THOUGHT ———————————

Great communicators talk less, not more. They convey their message with an economy of words delivered in a clear, concise manner. I find myself paying a lot more attention and remembering more of the conversation when I'm not the recipient of a long discourse given in a nonsensical manner

——————————— IN OTHER WORDS ———————————

The true spirit of conversation consists in
building on another man's observation, not overturning it.
~ Edward Bulwer-Lytton

I like to listen. I have learned a great deal from
listening carefully. Most people never listen.
~ Ernest Hemingway

*Most people do not listen with the intent to understand,
rather they listen with the intent to reply. They are busy
filtering everything through their own perspectives rather
than trying to understand another's frame of reference.*
~ Stephen R. Covey

*Your ability to communicate is the single most important skill
determining your success in every aspect of your life. You
dare not make the mistake of thinking that communication is
nothing but dumping information on another person.*
~ Bert Decker

*The listener has nearly as big a responsibility as the speaker
does… It's not a passive act, not if you want to do it right.*
~ Seth Godin

*Listening is a skill that has a dreadfully limited number
of truly effective practitioners. We are not taught
to listen in school, at home, or at work.*
~ Ben Joyce

*Wisdom is the reward you get for a lifetime of listening
when you'd have preferred to talk."*
~ Doug Larson

*Communication is something so simple and difficult
that we can never put it in simple words.*
~ T.S. Matthews

*Most conversations are simply monologues
delivered in the presence of witnesses.*
~ Margaret Millar

Silence is one of the great arts of conversation.
~ Hannah More

Talk low, talk slow, and don't say too much.
~ John Wayne

Listening is a reciprocal process –
we become more attentive to others if they have attended to us.
~ Margaret J. Wheatley

The key to communication is to
speak without offending and listen without defending.
~ Montel Williams

Composure: Keeping Your Cool

*Always keep your composure. You can't score from
the penalty box; and to win, you have to score.*
~ Bobby Hull

I realize you're much too young to remember Bobby Hull. Come to think of it, I'm almost too young to remember him myself. Unless you happen to be a hockey fan, you've probably never even heard of him.

Canadian-born Robert Marvin "Bobby" Hull was a professional ice hockey player, who played at that level for twenty-three years, and is widely considered to be among the best who ever played the game. Interestingly, other former players of that caliber include his son, Brett, who retired in 2005 after his own illustrious career.

Clearly, ice hockey was embedded in the Hull family DNA. Bobby and Brett are the only father-son duo to have ever won the sport's two most prestigious individual awards. They're also the only father and son pair to have each scored more than fifty goals during a single National Hockey League (NHL) season, and more than six hundred goals during their NHL careers.

Add Bobby's younger brother Dennis to the mix – more than three hundred NHL goals scored – and you have two generations of one family who scored in excess of fifteen hundred goals. And that's in a typically low-scoring sport, where more than three goals by a team in one game is rather high.

The two individual awards I mentioned are the Hart Memorial Trophy – awarded annually to the league's Most Valuable Player – and the Lady Byng Memorial Trophy, which brings us to the lesson for today.

As you know, the quote I used above included the word "composure," which for anyone who has ever watched a hockey game seems utterly absurd. It's a rough-and-tumble sport, with bodies flying everywhere, and with players frequently dropping their gloves and battling one another with great gusto. Rare is the game that lacks less than a few trips to the penalty box by players from both teams.

The Lady Byng Memorial Trophy is awarded to the player who, during an entire season, has been "adjudged to have exhibited the best type of sportsmanship and gentlemanly conduct combined with a high standard of playing ability." While Bobby Hull logged a significant number of minutes in a penalty box during his career, his conduct during at least one season was gentlemanly enough to merit that award.

I'm unaware of what records may be kept of runners-up for that award, but Hull apparently took his own advice – quoted above – seriously enough to have passed it on to the next generation. Following the 1989-90 season, son Brett took home his own Lady Byng Trophy, exactly twenty-five years after his father had done so.

Whether you call it composure, calmness, serenity – or more informally – chillin' out, hangin' loose, being cool as a cucumber, or whatever the latest acronym or abbreviation might be, it's a worthwhile quality to develop. It's hard to think or act clearly when you're worried or angry, and you often wind up regretting what you say or do when you've lost your cool.

The Donkey in the Well

There's a great story that's been making the rounds on the Internet for several years now that illustrates the value of calmness, even in difficult circumstances. There's no clue as to its author, but it's about a farmer and his faithful old donkey, which fell into a deep well one day. The farmer came running when he heard its cries but, in the darkness of the well, he couldn't see it, nor figure out how to get it out.

Its cries brought several neighbors over, but no one could think of a way to rescue that donkey. Finally, it was decided that the best and only course of action would be to put the donkey out of its misery by burying it and filling up that old well. So the neighbors took their shovels and starting filling up the well. At first, the donkey's cries intensified, but then they stopped completely.

No one understood why, until someone brought a light and held it over the well. When the farmer looked down in it, he saw his donkey standing calmly. Each time a shovelful of dirt landed on him, he simply shook it off. As the well gradually filled, that smart donkey simply stepped on top of each load of dirt, as if on a slow-moving elevator. When he reached ground level, he simply jumped out and happily trotted away.

Depending on which version you happen to read, it usually ends with a lesson one can draw from it. But my favorite ending simply says that "the donkey later came back and kicked the crap out of the farmer for trying to bury it."

But there are some valuable takeaways in this little fable. For me, the most important one is that, no matter how deep a hole you may be in, and how much dirt people throw at you and on you, the best approach is to remain cool, calm, and collected. That will help you figure out the best way to rescue yourself from your predicament.

Beware: A Millennium Approaches!

This happened more recently but, unless you're at least in your late teens, you probably don't remember it, or ever heard of it. As the year 1999 moved day-by-day to its conclusion, the world was about to face something no living person had ever experienced or would ever experience again. A thousand-year period – a millennium – was about to end, and to be replaced by a new one.

At the time, there were two theories about when that would actually take place. One large contingent held that it would be at midnight on December 31, 1999. Another large one argued that the outgoing thousand-year period wouldn't end until the last day of 2000. I won't bore you with the details about either side of the argument, because it's not important to this story.

What had caused widespread panic in both camps was the fact that, with dates, nearly all the world's computers were programmed to abbreviate the year, showing only the last two digits. When 1999 was to bid us farewell, would the year revert to 1900? No one knew what to expect. Would Y2K, as it was called, cause widespread disruption and confusion? I remember I was working an overnight shift in this little emergency department. As the seconds ticked across midnight, we all held our breath expecting the computers to shut down and the patient monitors to go into error mode.

Would the time-operated locks on bank vaults suddenly cease to function, blocking us from the funds we'd need? Would trains stop running? Should every aircraft in the world be grounded as the moment approached, in order to keep them from dropping like rain from the skies? Would our gas and electric and water utilities grind to a halt? Would worldwide lawlessness and looting become the order of the day?

In extreme cases, people began buying and hoarding huge quantities of food and other necessities of life. Some who lacked space to hold them bought large storage sheds to meet the need. Sales of hot tubs and Jacuzzis rose, not for bathing but for water storage. Then came another wave of buying, this time of guns and ammunition, to be used for protection against the looters who had failed to take the necessary precautions.

Such extreme measures were relatively limited and, for the most part, people went on with life as usual, confident that wiser heads had recognized the possible consequences of the date changes and had taken the necessary steps to minimize, or eliminate, the chances of widespread disruption.

Such panicky overreaction seems utterly absurd now, but that can happen when we venture into the unknown, and allow our worries to overtake our common sense. In December 2009, reporter Tony Long, writing in *Wired*, took a look back at the uproar. In an article headlined: *Dec. 31, 1999: Horror or Hype? Y2K Arrives and World Trembles*, he wrote: "If the threat was real – and there are plenty of people around who say it was – then the precautions paid off. If Y2K was a form of mass paranoia – and plenty of people believe that too – then a lot of money was wasted." In my little corner of the world, in the emergency department, everyone lived to see the morning. Some had worse headaches than others!

FOOD FOR THOUGHT

You may not have faced any crises so far, but there well may be some waiting for you in your journey through life, and your wellbeing may depend in large measure on how you face them. I've faced many of them in my life but many others I've worried about never happened.

In that article I just mentioned, Tony Long summed it up well, writing: "1999 passed into history with barely a whimper." All the panic, all the worry, had been for naught. It brought to mind the following bit of verse by an anonymous poet:

> *Oh, I worry over this thing and I worry over that,*
> *But I notice when the atmosphere has cleared,*
> *That the bad luck I had looked for*
> *Didn't come and knock me flat,*

And I didn't have the trouble that I feared.
Oh, I like to start the morning with an apprehensive sigh,
For I find a bit of worry to my taste;
But I cannot help a'thinking,
As the years go speeding by,
That an awful lot of worry goes to waste.

——— IN OTHER WORDS ———

Worry is the down payment on
90 percent of the trouble you won't have.

~ John Benton

Always behave like a duck – keep calm and unruffled on the
surface, but paddle like the devil underneath.

~ Jacob M. Braude

Rule number one is, don't sweat the small stuff.
Rule number two is, it's all small stuff.

~ Robert Eliot

Every day is the best day of the year.
He is rich who owns the day. And no one owns the day who
allows it to be invaded by fret and anxiety.

~ Ralph Waldo Emerson

I was always looking outside myself for strength and
confidence, but it comes from within. It is there all the time.

~ Anna Freud

You're only here for a short visit. Don't hurry. Don't worry.
And be sure to smell the flowers along the way.

~ Walter C. Hagen

Worriers spend a lot of time shoveling smoke.

~ Claude McDonald

*Stop worrying about the potholes in the road
and celebrate the journey!*
~ Barbara Hoffman

*You're going to have ups and downs all your life.
But if you don't learn to enjoy life even during the hard times,
you will never learn life for what it is.*
~ Charlie "Tremendous" Jones

*A man ninety years old was asked to what he attributed his
longevity. 'I reckon,' he said, with a twinkle in his eye,
'It's because most nights I went to bed and slept
when I should have sat up and worried.'*
~ Dorothea Kent

*Something I learned early is to not worry about what I can't
control. But what I can control is my attitude, my effort,
and my focus every single day.*
~ Tim Tebow

*Be content with what you have; rejoice in the way things are.
When you realize there is nothing lacking,
the whole world belongs to you.*
~ Lao Tzu

*Worry is like a rocking chair;
it keeps you moving but doesn't get you anywhere.*
~ Corrie ten Boom

An Attitude of Gratitude

*If you want to become great, you have to focus
on being grateful. You can change any situation in your life
by simply redirecting your mind to focus on
what's right about it versus what is wrong.*

~ Darren Hardy

Darren Hardy, whom I've quoted above, is the publisher and editorial director of *SUCCESS* magazine. In that role, he has the opportunity to meet regularly with high achievers in virtually every field of endeavor, and to learn what has taken them to the top – to become outliers.

The words I quoted are from a blog post he wrote, titled *To Be Great, Be Grateful*. In it, he points out that our brains are not wired to express gratitude. "Your brain," he writes, "has only one primary responsibility—to keep you alive. Thus, your brain is constantly on the lookout for danger and attack warnings. Your brain is programmed specifically to seek out the negative."

To counteract that natural tendency, Hardy presents his readers with this challenge: "Think of an area of your life you are having difficulty in and want to improve. For the next 21 days, take three minutes at the end of the day and write down what about that problematic situation you appreciate, what's good and what you're grateful for."

Three minutes a day for 21 days adds up to just over one hour – an hour that can literally change our lives.

As children, we're taught that expressing thanks for gifts we receive is the polite thing to do, that the presents we receive on our birthdays or at Christmas call for us to write "thank-you" notes to Grandma and Grandpa. So we do it, often grudgingly, not because we're truly grateful but because it's expected. But how much better it is when our gratitude comes from the heart and not from a sense of duty.

The Gratitude Experiment

Recently, I was introduced to a company with the curious name of SoulPancake. Founded in 2008, it's described as "a new media company that seeks to provide platforms to explore 'big-think' topics." One recent study was on the topic of "gratitude," and the degree to which it impacts the happiness level of grateful people. The study was part of a project titled "The Science of Happiness."

Each participant in the study was directed to write a letter of gratitude to someone who had been a major influence in his or her life, explaining why it was so important and how it had affected the writer. The next step in the exercise was for the participants to read their letters aloud. Then, with the cameras rolling, they were asked to call the individuals to whom they'd written and to read their heartfelt letters to them.

Watching their faces while they were making the calls was motivational enough for me and, predictably, the response from the recipients of the letters was very positive. However, the take-home point of the exercise was to demonstrate the impact it had on the letter writers themselves. The results showed conclusively, and demonstrably, that expressing gratitude can significantly increase one's level of happiness.

The Future, not the Past

A recent article in *The Huffington Post* further emphasizes the importance of gratitude going forward. It was written by David DeSteno, Ph.D., a professor at Northeastern University and a much-published author. He begins by acknowledging that expressing gratitude in some situations can be a chore (like writing those "thank-you" notes to Grandma). That reaction, he writes, "comes from a somewhat misguided view that gratitude is all about looking backward – back to what has already been. But in reality, that's not how gratitude truly works."

He goes on to describe a series of experiments his team conducted about gratitude, experiments that clearly show how "contagious" an attitude of gratitude can be. The conclusion: "The more gratitude people feel, the more likely it is they'll help anyone, even if it's someone they've never laid eyes on before."

DeSteno ended his article with these words: "Next time you have the opportunity to say 'thank you,' don't let it ring hollow. Embrace the gratitude; feel it as deeply as you can, because in so doing, you're actually increasing the odds that in the future we'll all have more for which to be grateful. On the deepest, unconscious level, gratitude is really about being grateful for the actions that are yet to come."

One Man's Approach

The late Charlie "Tremendous" Jones was one person who never let the opportunity to say "thank you" ring hollow. In fact, they were typically the first words he'd say when meeting someone. Whether it was a waiter, a cab driver, a flight attendant or a store clerk, Charlie's opening line would typically be, "Thank you for your smile." He was often asked, "But what if they're not smiling?" His reply: "Well, because I'd already thanked them, they'd realize they owed me one and would usually smile right back."

From 1965 until his death in 2008, Charlie Jones traveled the world as a professional speaker and humorist. During his career, he received virtually every honor in the speaking profession, and was ranked by his peers as one of the top fifty speakers of the twentieth century.

By the way, the nickname "Tremendous" wasn't his idea. "I realize it's a ridiculous nickname," he'd explain, "one that's been a source of embarrassment to me for years. It certainly isn't a nickname I chose, and I don't wear it because I've accomplished great things. No, the simple truth is that I acquired it solely because of a limited vocabulary.

"That's right! Early in my insurance career, whenever one of my agents would report that he or she had sold a policy, I'd respond, 'Tremendous!' Or when a young couple at church would announce the birth of their new baby or the purchase of their first home, my reply would invariably be 'Tremendous!' Even the colleague who told me his mother-in-law had just died was likely to hear 'Tremendous!' I used the word so often that it stuck, and I've never been able to get away from it or live it down."

My Gratitude Campaign

Years ago, for reasons I can't put my finger on, I realized how fortunate I've been and how a few select educators made a huge impact on my life. So I made it a point to track down and thank all of the influential teachers and professors in my life. It was phenomenally rewarding and I got more out of it than they did.

As a freshman at Drake University, I signed up for a class in Astronomy, which I incorrectly believed was little more than talking about and looking at some stars. Little did I know I'd signed up for a class that was essentially "Physics of Outer Space." Looking back, it probably wasn't that hard; however, at the time, it was a real challenge.

The physicist who taught it was named Professor Staunton. He later went on to become the Chair of the Physics Department at Drake. At the time I took it, I barely squeaked out a grade of a "C." Then, after my first semester, I finally started to develop some confidence in my abilities and began pulling up my grades. During my second year, I managed to surprise myself – and astonish my parents – by getting an "A" in all my classes. It was a great experience to build on, and I continued to do well throughout the rest of my time at Drake. By senior year, I had a pretty good science GPA; however, that "C" during my freshman year continued to drag it down a bit.

One day, I went back to talk to Professor Staunton (who had little memory of me). I found him in the basement of the Physics building in his office, which was also occupied by a really big and scary looking German Shepherd. The first thing the professor did when he saw me was look at the dog and say "Sic him!" Of course, that startled me a bit; although I wasn't the best student, I was always polite and respectful (at least to my teachers) and thought encouraging Cujo on me was a bit aggressive..

I recovered from my momentary shock of imagining I was going to turn into the "lunch of Cujo" and sat down to explain my plight. I was applying to medical school, and any "C," let alone a "C" in a science class, didn't look good on my transcripts. After listening to my story and my explanation about why I was asking him to turn my "C" into a "Pass" (Pass/Fail grades didn't count toward your GPA), he smiled and said, "Sure, no problem, and good luck!"

With that, the meeting was over. I walked out with all my limbs intact, no "C" on my report card (at least in science), and a slightly higher GPA. To this day, I'm not sure if that made the difference of me getting into medical school, but it definitely didn't hurt my chances.

Twenty-six years later, I caught up with him on the day he was packing up his office. He had just retired as Chair of the Department of Physics and as a college professor. I recounted what he did for me, what it meant to me and briefly told him what I was doing (I was on the Board of Trustees at Drake). Although he didn't remember changing my grade, he smiled and said he had a vague recollection of siccing his dog on me. I could tell that my thanking him for this – small to him yet huge to me – act of kindness, meant a lot to him. I consider myself very fortunate to have caught up with him on his last day of his distinguished career at Drake.

Most recently I tracked down Dr. Ted Booden, who was the Dean of Admissions for the medical school I attended. I was incredibly fortunate that he was the person who interviewed me. For whatever reason (I was a marginal applicant), he decided I'd be a good addition to the class and I found out later that he accepted me on the spot.

During the next four years, he and I became much closer. I was our class president during two of the years and when one of my peers wasn't living up to standards, he'd sit me down and proceed to "educate me" on how to "educate them." Dr. Booden was an amazing leader and mentor who affected the lives of millions of patients by educating thousands of medical students. Most importantly (at least to me) was his belief *in* me and I owe him a lifelong debt of gratitude.

These events taught me two things: show gratitude – it's often these simple, little gestures which are the most meaningful to others. Second, treat everyone with kindness. You don't know the profound, lasting effect your simple act of kindness could have on that person or on humanity.

Mackay's Moral

Harvey Mackay is a well-known and successful businessman and author. He's the founder and chairman of MackayMitchell Envelope Company, has written five best-selling business books, and writes a widely syndicated weekly newspaper column. On more than one occasion, he's written about the importance of gratitude, and has lamented what he sees as a decline in the use of the words "thank you."

In one column, dated October 9, 2008, he related an incident David Letterman had featured on his TV show. A viewer had described his experience on a shopping trip to a retail store. Unable to get anyone's attention, he finally found the items he needed. When the cashier rang up the sale, she bagged his items and abruptly handed him his receipt without saying a word. As he was leaving, he said: "A 'thank you' would have been nice," to which she rudely replied: "It's printed on your receipt."

Mackay always ends his column with "Mackay's Moral." This one's moral read: "Thank U is a college from which we should never graduate." Well said!

FOOD FOR THOUGHT

Stay grateful – take nothing for granted. It is the rare individual whose success cannot be attributed – at least in part – to the kindness of others.

Go back and express gratitude to those who helped you along your path. It will make a difference in their lives and it will make a profound difference in yours.

IN OTHER WORDS

Gratitude makes sense of our past, brings peace for today,
and creates a vision for tomorrow.
~ Melody Beattie

When it comes to life the critical thing is whether you
take things for granted or take them with gratitude.
~ Gilbert Keith Chesterton

Gratitude is riches. Complaining is poverty.
Instead of complaining about what's wrong,
be grateful for what's right.
~ Zachary Fisher

An attitude of gratitude flavors everything you do.
Learning to be thankful is the golden thread
woven through every truly successful life.
~ Charlie "Tremendous" Jones

Let us be grateful to people who make us happy,
they are the charming gardeners who make our souls blossom.
~ Marcel Proust

Thankfulness for me is not so much an enthusiastic response to
good and pleasant things in my life as it is a disciplined way
of viewing life. To do this requires practice, practice, practice.
~ Bob Snyder

He who forgets the language of gratitude
can never be on speaking terms with happiness.
~ C. Neil Strait

Gratitude is a currency that we can mint for ourselves,
and spend without fear of bankruptcy.
~ Fred De Witt Van Amburgh

Feeling gratitude and not expressing it is like
wrapping a present and not giving it.
~ William Arthur Ward

The more you recognize and express gratitude
for the things you have, the more things
you will have to express gratitude for.
~ Zig Ziglar

Through a Different Lens

*An innovative insight is not the product of an individual's
brilliance. It's not as if innovators' heads are wired
in different ways. Innovation typically comes from looking at
the world through a slightly different lens.*

~ Gary Hamel

Dr. Gary Hamel is a well-known consultant and management expert who has long been a champion of innovation. At the same time, he's been an outspoken critic of business leaders who steadfastly refuse to embrace the concept, preferring instead to continue doing what they've always done.

In a *Forbes* magazine article in December 2012, he wrote: "A huge amount has been talked about and written on innovation over the last ten years or so. Most of us understand that innovation is enormously important. It's the only insurance against irrelevance."

A few years earlier, writing in *Harvard Business Review* (Feb. 2009), he posed these questions: "Why should organizations be so much better at operating than they are at innovating? Why should so many people work in uninspiring companies? Surely we can do better."

Well, I'm happy to report that, in many circles, and particularly among teenagers and other young men and women, we are doing better. I'm going to share some exciting examples of innovation with you, but let me begin with my first attempt at breaking out of the "we've-always-done-it-this-way" box, and trying something different.

When I was 13, I loved to fly kites. I built and flew all sorts of them, from box kites to two-stick square kites. Most of these kites were tethered to a roll of store-bought string and only went a few hundred feet in the sky. My friend Jeff, who was a lot smarter and did better in school than I did, had a great time "dog fighting" kites and retrieving them from trees. However, it wasn't enough.

At some point, we learned about a group attempting to set the world altitude record for kites and thought "How hard can this be?" So we found and somehow convinced a string manufacturer to give us 36,000 feet of 80-pound test string. (For those keeping score at home, that's nearly seven miles of string.) We designed and then built a mount with a hand crank so we could easily rewind the string. We even attached the mount to an electric drill so we wouldn't have to hand crank the string and the kite back to earth.

After a few practice runs, Jeff and I decided to go for the world record, which we learned was an altitude of 31,000 feet. We'd both been watching the weather on our local news channel. We picked a day when the weather was predicted to be optimal: a warm early fall day with a breeze out of the west. As it turned out, the weather was inexplicably perfect (weather forecasters in Chicago were generally and almost invariably wrong).

That afternoon, we went back to my house, gathered the apparatus, and walked over to a nearby school, where we launched what we believed would be our entry for the new world record for altitude for a kite.

The apparatus we created worked beautifully and the kite quickly unwound about one-third of the string. The challenge was that, although it was using up a lot of string, the kite was only about 300 feet in the air. It went out, but it didn't go up. For some reason, it had never occurred to us that the kite would go anywhere but up. Although we were a bit dismayed and somewhat perplexed, we remained undeterred from our quest for kite fame and fortune.

We decided that we'd change directions and achieve the world record for how far a kite could travel while still tethered. If we couldn't go high, we could still go far. Now that we were back in record setting mood, the string continued to unwind until about one-half of it was gone. We were on the way into the Guinness Book!

At this point, we could no longer see the kite, not even with binoculars. We believed we had let it out about three or four miles but, judging by the angle of the string as it came out of the apparatus, it seemed to be only about 500 feet in the air. Also, we had to physically unwind the string, using the crank. If we used the drill and let out the string too fast, the angle of the trajectory became more shallow and we feared the dreaded power lines or tall trees.

All of a sudden, after we'd been standing there for about an hour, trying to set the world record, the string went slack and settled to the ground. We hadn't seen the kite itself for about 30 minutes but still felt the tension in the string and were still imagining that all of a sudden the kite would soar into the heavens directly about our head. Not so much. Instead, we had about four miles of unwound string lying on the ground.

For about 10 seconds, we tried to roll it back up, using the drill connected to the crank assembly. The first time, we ran into some friction, the string went taut, the drill caught, and the motor started spewing out blue smoke. We decided to cut the string and our losses, collected the extension cord and what was left of the apparatus, and now with a much smaller roll of string, we sulked our way home.

Of course, I got over it, but that setback did nothing to dampen my enthusiasm for innovation, which, despite some modest successes and a few spectacular failures, continues unabated to this day.

A Whole New Ball Game

This story begins in the backyard of the Mullany family in Fairfield, Connecticut. It was the summer of 1953 and 12-year-old Dave Mullany was playing ball with a friend, using a plastic golf ball and a broom handle. The backyard was too small for them to use real baseballs, and they kept trying to throw curves with the golf ball, but it refused to cooperate. That's when Dave's father, also named Dave, got involved.

It was a weekday and the only reason he was home that afternoon was because his business had recently failed and he hadn't been able to find a job. Seeing the boys' frustration, he decided to try and help. A friend of his worked at a nearby factory which made various packaging products, including a plastic ball-shaped one used to package small perfume bottles. Father Dave got several samples and, with young Dave's help, started experimenting.

Using razor blades and some tape, they cut each of the "balls" in half and began cutting holes of varying shapes and sizes in them before taping two halves back together and testing them, finally settling on a product that would curve when thrown. When his dad asked what the boys had been calling their game, young Dave replied "whiff," referring to the sound a baseball bat (or a golf club) makes when swinging at, and missing, the ball.

The father and son team quickly decided to drop the letter "h," and add two other letters. Thus was born the Wiffle Ball. Today, some 60 years later, WIFFLE Balls (the trademarked name) are played in backyards all across America and in many other countries. The company is still family-owned and is led by another Dave Mullany, the son and grandson of the two who started it all by looking through a different lens.

From Containers to Clinics

They're familiar sights everywhere we travel: railroad trains comprised of one hundred or more flatcars stacked with large shipping containers and headed to, or from, various seaports around the world. When they were introduced in the mid-20th century, these large rectangular steel containers themselves represented what was an innovative approach to the shipment of freight. Instead of the wide variety in the shapes and sizes that had been customary, their uniform size and shape made it easy, and more secure, to transfer large amounts of freight among various modes of transportation, including trains, trucks and ships.

Often, when containers are, for whatever reason, no longer needed, they're abandoned and can be seen sitting on unused railroad sidings, typically covered with the handiwork of graffiti "artists." But Gabrielle Palermo, Susanna Young, and their fellow students at Arizona State University, James Tyler and John Walters, saw these abandoned containers through a different lens.

What they saw were potential medical clinics for use in developing countries! I read about what they were doing and reached out to offer assistance. Since I'd already made every mistake in the medical clinic playbook, I figured at the very least, I could share with them what not to do. The more I learned, the more I liked.

When Gabrielle enrolled at ASU in 2009, she had planned on becoming a doctor, but her focus changed when she learned of the plight of young pregnant women in Kenya where, of 100,000 live births, 530 of the mothers did not survive. "I wanted to be a doctor, but that changed when I went into this process," she says. "It's now my passion. I love creating a business that will help save lives."

To turn their vision into reality, the four engineering students formed a new company called G3Box, to redesign and equip these recycled containers into medical clinics. The first of these units, a maternity clinic, was completed in early 2013 and shipped to Kenya, to be staffed by local doctors and nurses. The team projects that if only four young women are seen daily, many lives, of both mothers and babies, will be saved each year.

A Medical Breakthrough

Jack Andraka is, among other things, a scientist, an inventor and a cancer researcher. His most noteworthy accomplishment to date has resulted from his involvement in all three of these disciplines. While the final results are still subject to years of testing and research, Andraka has developed a simple and inexpensive method of early detection of one of the world's deadliest diseases – pancreatic cancer.

To date, medical technology has been unable to accurately diagnose the disease in its early stages. By the time it's detected, it has nearly always spread to the point where the patient is unlikely to survive. The annual death toll from this lethal disease is about 40,000, with a five-year survival rate of less than six percent.

Spurred on by the death of a close family friend from pancreatic cancer, Andraka began intense study and research of the disease, with the goal of finding a means of early detection, when the chances of survival would be high. After conducting some early experiments, he sent his findings to about two hundred researchers. Only one, a professor of the Johns Hopkins School of Medicine, responded favorably.

For the next several months, under that professor's watchful eye, Andraka spent countless hours in the lab, testing and experimenting again and again. He discovered that a higher than normal amount of a protein called mesothelin in the blood was the red flag he'd been looking for. He came up with a simple and accurate method of detection, similar to the device used in diabetes testing. Laboratory testing in mice confirmed the accuracy of his discovery.

Recognition came quickly. Andraka received the 2012 Gordon E. Moore Award, a $75,000 prize given by Intel that honors the company's co-founder. He was also named the winner of the Smithsonian Ingenuity Award and was invited to speak at a prestigious TED conference. During his TED Talk, titled "Bring on the Medical Revolution," he claimed that technology in medicine "has stagnated," and spoke about the need for more innovation in that field.

Toward the end of his message, he made an appeal for more teenagers to get involved, claiming that "teens are the epitome of creativity." While that may seem an odd statement at first, Jack Andraka himself is well qualified to make it. At the time he won the Intel award, he was a high school freshman and, as I write these words, he's 17 years old!

In describing his research to the TED audience, he noted that when he began, "I didn't even know I had a pancreas." But that didn't stop him. There's probably never before been the opportunity that exists today, with virtually all the world's information literally at your fingertips. All it takes is "looking at the world through a slightly different lens."

FOOD FOR THOUGHT

When attempting to do the impossible, pick good people, prepare as best you can, and then be willing to adapt to unforeseen changes.

Anyone can change the world: Some of the largest, best companies and greatest new ideas come from young adults who are not afraid to see the world differently, take risks, work hard, and come up with new ways to improve the world.

IN OTHER WORDS

The creative is the place where no one else has ever been. You have to leave the city of your comfort and go into the wilderness of your intuition. You can't get there by bus, only by hard work and risk and by not quite knowing what you're doing.

~ Alan Alda

*Why not upset the apple cart? If you don't,
the apples will rot anyway.*

~ Frank A. Clark

Innovation comes from seeing the world as opportunity.

~ Jamie Coughlin

Creativity requires the freedom to consider 'unthinkable' alternatives, to doubt the worth of cherished practices.

~ John W. Gardner

It would be a great mistake to confine your imagination to the way things have always been done.

~ Harold Geneen

Innovation is often the act of taking something that worked over there and using it over here.

~ Seth Godin

Sometimes when you innovate you make mistakes. It is best to admit them quickly and get on with improving your other innovations.

~ Steve Jobs

Take an object. Do something to it. Do something else to it.

~ Jasper Johns

There is a gold mine within you from which you can extract everything you need to live life gloriously, joyously, and abundantly.

~ Joseph Murphy

You've gotta be original, because if you're like someone else, what do they need you for?

~ Bernadette Peters

I have always been driven to buck the system, to innovate, to take things beyond where they've been.

~ Sam Walton

Throughout the ages, innovation has been fostered by imagining what is possible instead of what you can do with your current resources. The key way to innovate is to question the status quo and 'ask the right questions'—not what can we do now, but what is possible.

~ Todd Rhoades

The Positive Power of Peers

Be careful where you stop to inquire for directions along the road of life. Wise is the person who fortifies his life with the right friendships. If you run with wolves, you will learn how to howl. But, if you associate with eagles, you will learn how to soar to great heights.

~ General Colin Powell

Those words from General Powell echo some sound advice that dates back perhaps three thousand years or more. King Solomon, who reigned over Israel nearly a thousand years before Christ's birth, put it this way, as recorded in the Old Testament Book of Proverbs: "The one who walks with the wise grows wise, but a companion of fools suffers harm."

You may have heard it expressed as "Birds of a feather flock together," which dates back to the 16th century, or the more recent "You're known by the company you keep." Country music star Dolly Parton wrote and recorded a song titled "The Company You Keep." It includes these lyrics: "You'd better look before you leap / 'Cause you're getting' in too deep …/ The road of life is steep / And you're known by the company you keep."

OK, you get the picture. So where do you stand? Do you hang with wolves – or eagles? Are you walking with the wise? Or are you heading down that steep road Dolly sang about? It's called "peer pressure," and the choices you're making today could impact the rest of your life, and the lives of many others – for better or for worse.

A Look Back

A couple of hundred years ago, a certain man wrote a letter to his grandson. It included these words:

> *When I recollect that at 14 years of age the whole care and direction of myself was thrown on my self entirely, without a relative or friend qualified to advise or guide me, and recollect the various sorts of bad company with which I associated from time to time, I am astonished I did not turn off with some of them, and become as worthless to society as they were. I had the good fortune to become acquainted very early with some characters of very high standing, and to feel the incessant wish that I could even become what they were.*

The path he chose turned out to be a good one indeed. He became an excellent student, graduating from the College of William and Mary in Virginia. Along the way, he learned five languages and showed strong interest in such disciplines as science, architecture, and philosophy. His adult roles included service as Governor of Virginia, U.S. Minister to France, and Secretary of State. At the time he wrote that letter to his grandson, he was nearing the end of his second term as President of the United States. His name was Thomas Jefferson.

He was, of course, one of our nation's Founding Fathers, the primary author of the Declaration of Independence, and our third President. At age 65, at the height of his enormously successful career, he credited that success to a choice he'd made as a boy, telling his grandson it was because of his "good fortune to become acquainted very early with some characters of very high standing, and to feel the incessant wish that I could become what they were." Jefferson had chosen his peers wisely, and the lessons he'd learned from them as a teenager would impact the rest of his life -- in a positive way.

Another View

It's been well established that peers can and do have significant impact on our lives. Unfortunately, that impact can be negative, as well as positive. Among the former is bullying. Although it's been practiced in varying degrees throughout history, the growth of social media seems to have made it more widespread, notorious – and even deadly. According to one report, as many as 160,000 students skip school every day because facing the bullying has become unbearable.

The practice even has a relatively new term: cyberbullying, giving those who indulge in it ever-widening access to audiences for their cruelty. When even one instance is too many, we're hearing story after story of teenagers taking their own lives, driven to that extreme by the vicious attacks of their peers.

But, as Thomas Jefferson illustrated so powerfully, the power of peer groups can be – and often is – a major force for good. In a 2010 magazine article titled "Teen Peer Groups can be a positive influence," clinical psychologist Val Farmer made a strong case for their value. While acknowledging and describing the negative side, he wrote: "Children learn to evaluate themselves through the eyes of their peers. They get important feedback on their personal characteristics. They practice and gain social skills and confidence. They learn fairness, cooperation and how to defer personal gratification to group goals."

He goes on to describe the role education plays among peer groups, noting that: "Positive peer groups usually have strong bonds to school while negative groups are anti-education in some fashion."

A Chain Reaction

I can't think of a more vivid example of that truth than an event that occurred on April 20, 1999, sending shock waves all across the country and around the world. It was late morning on a Friday when two unhappy students at Columbine High School in Colorado entered the school, launching an attack that would result in the murder of twelve students and one teacher, and then the suicides of the attackers, Eric Harris and Dylan Klebold.

Harris and Klebold had long shown evidence of discontent, and had been aided and abetted by a few classmates and peers in obtaining the weapons used in the savage crime. It's little wonder that, in his magazine article, Farmer wrote: "The public has a tendency to associate teen peer group influence as only negative."

But can there be a positive side to what happened at Columbine? Well, consider the story of Rachel Scott. A classmate of the killers, she was their first victim, shot four times and killed instantly. She had known Klebold since their kindergarten days, and they'd shared the same classes until the day they died. But what different paths their lives had taken. He had joined the wolfpack, while Rachel preferred the company of eagles.

Shortly before her death, she had written: "I have this theory that if one person can go out of their way to show compassion, then it will start a chain reaction of the same." Inspired by her words and drawings, her father and stepmother began a movement called Rachel's Challenge. Its mission: "To inspire, equip and empower every person to create a permanent, positive cultural change in their school, business and community by starting a chain reaction of kindness and compassion."

According to its website, www.rachelschallenge.org, Rachel's message has reached more than 19 million people, with two million more added every year. Not surprisingly, it has had a major impact on students – her peers. The website reports: "In one survey, seventy-eight percent of students indicated they would definitely intervene in a bullying incident in their school after seeing Rachel's Challenge. In the last three years, Rachel's Challenge has received nearly 500 unsolicited emails from students stating that after hearing Rachel's story they reached out for help as they were contemplating suicide. Some even state that 'Rachel saved my life.'"

A Close Call

I've been very lucky over the years to have selected friends and groups that have had positive, enduring effects on my life. For whatever reason, likely good parenting, I was able to stay away from those experimenting with drugs or alcohol. Don't get me wrong; I wasn't perfect while growing up – far from it. However, I was blessed not to have to endure the pain and suffering which goes along with using illicit substances.

I did have one close call! I spent a ton of time at the home of a nearby family. Our backyards were kitty-corner from each other. They were great parents, with four kids, three of whom were around my age; it was my home away from home. Mike, the oldest of the siblings, was the leader of the neighborhood while growing up. A great guy, he was a bit like an abusive (in a good way) big brother. After all, I was used to being smacked around by my by older sister, so what was one more person who took pleasure in "teaching" me?

One day, several of us were playing basketball on their driveway. Mike's friend Bill was part of the pickup game. Between games, he motioned everyone into the garage and pulled out what was reportedly a "joint." Mind you, up until that moment, I'd never seen marijuana, so, for all I knew, it could have been broccoli leaves, or some other innocuous substance. However, everyone else seemed to know what it was, so I pretended I did too. After a few minutes of questions and answers, Bill proceeded to light it and start smoking it. I do remember the smell, which was strangely both sweet and pungent.

I also knew there was no way I was going to put that thing in my mouth. All of a sudden, Bill, who was bigger than I was, grabbed me around the neck in a headlock and proceeded to try to hold the tip of the joint against my lips. Now, I don't want to sound like Bill Clinton, but I actually did hold my breath and didn't inhale. Parenthetically,

Bill's last name was Roach. Oh, the irony of almost being forced to smoke pot by a guy whose last name is synonymous for a joint!

You can *always* tell the quality of a person by the people with whom he or she associates. So, if your peer group is comprised of people whose behavior leaves much to be desired, you may want to rethink your choices. I know it's very hard to change your peer group; you'll likely be teased or even ridiculed. Changing doesn't mean you don't care about them, it simply means that, at least for now, you've decided to spend your precious time with friends who make better choices and will encourage and support your efforts to soar!

———————— FOOD FOR THOUGHT ————————

Fair or not, you are judged by the friends you keep and whether you like it or not, your friends' ideals, motivations, and actions will to some degree rub off on you. Although you can't choose your family, you can choose your friends and these friends will ultimately be extremely influential – maybe as influential as your family members – so choose wisely.

IN OTHER WORDS

Nothing in this world appeases loneliness as does a flock of friends! …There is always at least one who will understand, inspire, and give you the lift you may need at the time. Fortify yourself with a flock of friends.
~ George Matthew Adams

Learn a lesson from the snowflake. Tiny and fragile – but look what happens when they stick together.
~ Ben Blanton

Alone we can do so little, together we can do so much."
~ Helen Keller

Call it a clan, call it a network, call it a tribe, call it a family.
Whatever you call it, whoever you are, you need one.
~ Jane Temple Howard

You have to go into a challenge as a person of hope,
or nothing is going to happen. If you can envision it, you can
help other folks envision it, and together you can get there.
~ Rosemary Agneessens

A dream you dream alone is only a dream.
A dream you dream together is reality.
~ John Lennon

The quality of your life is determined by
the quality of your relationships.
~ Harvey Mackay

The possibility for rich relationships exists all around you – you
simply have to open your eyes, open your mouth
and most importantly, open your heart.
~ Cheryl Richardson

In every person who comes near you look for what is good and
strong; honor that; try to imitate it, and your faults will drop
off like dead leaves when their time comes.
~ John Ruskin

Some would argue that you're as successful
as the company you keep. Certainly there is
a connection between our friends and who we are.
~ Simon Sinek

We cannot hold a torch to light another's path
without brightening our own.
~ Ben Sweetland

*When we seek for connection, we restore the world
to wholeness. Our seemingly separate lives become meaningful
as we discover how truly necessary we are to each other.*
~ Margaret Wheatley

*Lots of people want to ride with you in the limo,
but what you want is someone who will take
the bus with you when the limo breaks down.*
~ Oprah Winfrey

The Mentor:
Helping Others Realize Their Dreams

Share your success and help others succeed.
Give everyone a chance to have a piece of the pie.
If the pie's not big enough, make a bigger pie.
~ Dave Thomas

Unless you're at least in your early twenties, you may not recognize the above name or know anything about the man himself. But chances are good that you've visited one or more of the outlets run by the company he founded.

From 1989 until his death in 2002, Dave Thomas was perhaps the most recognized and admired TV spokesman in America. During that period, he appeared in hundreds of low-key and humorous commercials representing Wendy's, the chain of restaurants he had founded in 1969. He had chosen the name "Wendy's" in honor of one of his daughters.

The quotation I used above includes a word that represents both his passion and his legacy – Others! Yet, there was little about his early life that would seem to point him in that direction. Born in New Jersey, he'd been adopted at six weeks of age and never knew his birth parents. When he was five, his adoptive mother died and he spent the next several years either with his grandmother in Michigan or moving often with his father as the latter sought work. When he was 12, he got his first job, working as a busboy in a Knoxville, Tennessee restaurant. But it didn't last long, as an argument with his boss cost him his job. He vowed then that he'd never lose another job.

Father and son kept on the move, landing at one point in Fort Wayne, Indiana. Dave was 15 when he went to work at another restaurant. Then, when his father announced yet another move, Dave had had enough. He dropped out of high school and began working full-time at the restaurant. Except for the career field he was in, there was still little to suggest what the future would hold for this 15-year-old high school dropout. Later, he would often mention that quitting school was the biggest mistake of his life and, at age 61, he finally earned his diploma.

When the Korean War broke out in 1950, Dave enlisted in the U.S. Army. Then, following his discharge in 1953, he returned to the Fort Wayne restaurant. While there, he had the opportunity to meet and to work with Colonel Harland Sanders, founder of the Kentucky Fried Chicken chain. Throughout his career, he would often give credit to Colonel Sanders for his kindness in mentoring him, and for the successful career that would follow.

In 1969, in Columbus, Ohio, Dave opened the first Wendy's Restaurant. It marked the start of what would become the nation's third-largest hamburger restaurant chain, with more than 6,000 locations. Dave stepped out of active management of the company in 1982, but continued in his role as its main spokesman until his death. Despite his fame, he never let it go to his head, insisting he was simply "a hamburger cook."

But he never forgot the lessons he had learned along the road to success. His lack of education as a teenager had taught him its importance. After earning his diploma at Coconut Creek High School in south Florida, he launched the Dave Thomas Education Center in that community. It includes both a Middle School Academy and an Alternative High School, aimed at meeting the needs of at-risk youth and teen parents. Thanks to the kindness and generosity of Dave Thomas, there is no cost to attend either facility.

Yet, his focus on others goes well beyond education. Dave never forgot the fact that he'd been adopted but, for a long time, he preferred not to talk about it. When a TV interviewer encouraged him to do so, he replied that he would, "if I could just help one boy or one girl get a home."

In 1990, President George H.W. Bush asked him to become the spokesman for a national campaign to arouse adoption awareness. He not only accepted but, two years later, he established the Dave Thomas Foundation for Adoption. A public charity, its primary goal is: "to help every child in foster care find a loving, permanent family."

The foundation lost its champion in 2002 when Dave Thomas died, but it continues the legacy he left – that one word, Others! Launched in 2004, its Wendy's Wonderful Kids program is a partnership with Wendy's restaurants that funds adoption professionals to find families for children in foster care. Within two years, the program had expanded to every state in the U.S., the District of Columbia, and two Canadian provinces.

Dave Thomas once said: "Only in America would a guy like me, from humble beginnings and without a high school diploma, become successful. America gave me a chance to live the life I want and work to make my dreams come true. We should never take our freedoms for granted, and we should seize every opportunity presented to us." Those opportunities still exist, to a much greater degree than they did when he was a teenager.

If you'd like to find a mentor, the best advice I can offer comes from Dave Thomas himself: "Instead of waiting for someone to take you under his wing, go out and find a wing to climb under." I never knew Dave Thomas but, having been adopted myself, I feel a special kinship with him.

The Mentor's Role

I've been asked on occasion to describe what a mentor is, and what he or she does in that role. Well, let's start by listing a few similar names for that word: coach, teacher, guide, advisor, counselor, role model. During the mentoring relationship, the mentor may play all or most of those roles at varying times and in varying situations. Here's how Oprah Winfrey defined it: "A mentor is someone who allows you to see the hope inside yourself."

In college and again in medical school, I was a member of the Big Brothers Big Sisters organization. In college, I was paired up with a nice kid named Tommy, who was being raised by a single parent. But until this point, he lacked a "stable" (if they only knew) male influence. I never had a little brother, so hanging out with Tommy was as much fun for me as I hope it was for him.

While in medical school, I was paired with a pre-teenager named Chris. Chris had some challenges. He was socially awkward as a result of his congenital cleft palate and lip. He had multiple surgeries to correct this and although the roof of his mouth was repaired, his upper lip was noticeably deformed. Despite his challenges, Chris was a real trouper. He didn't complain, was up for everything, and had a great heart. Once he entered his teenage years and made some new friends, we drifted apart. To this day, I wonder what happened to him and have tried to cyber-find him without any success.

During those years, I promised myself I'd mentor anyone who asked (and some who didn't) in whatever ways I could, to offer up any knowledge or in the very least, tell them all the ways I screwed it up.

Kelly was a junior in high school who wanted to become a doctor. I was introduced to her by our marketing director, who was very active in a great organization called Young Life. Once I got to know Kelly, she told me she'd been headed down the wrong path with the wrong group of friends and made a conscious effort to change her peer group, so she joined Young Life.

Kelly was, in a word, fearless. She learned to fly at 16, did well in school, and was accepted to a private college where she continued to excel. While on breaks, she'd hang out in the emergency department with me and soak up anything she could. I took her on a SWAT training mission where she dressed up in body armor, was given a rifle, and placed in a bus as the armed assailant. She was told to shoot any officers who approached her with simunition (essentially a low velocity, paint-tipped bullet).

For reasons I don't want to think about, when shooting the officers who were assaulting the bus, she'd hit them in the crotch, earning her a nickname I won't disclose. Kelly survived her make-believe terrorist bus hostage drill to go on to graduate from college, get married, and apply and get accepted to medical school. She and I wrote a number of articles together, and we stay in touch to this day.

One of my proudest memories was watching her walk across the stage during the White Coat Ceremony marking the transition from her pre-clinical to clinical studies during her first week of medical school. It gives me great satisfaction to know Kelly will go on, in her humble yet fearless way, to care for her patients, change the world, and impact and mentor a whole new generation of doctors who, in turn, will repeat it.

For me, mentoring, and the kindness shown while engaged in it, harkens back to an earlier era. It's been more than three hundred years since famed English scientist Sir Isaac Newton wrote, in a letter to a colleague, "If I have seen farther it is by standing on the shoulders of giants." I would echo those words today. If, for a few people, I can be a metaphorical "giant" and because of this, others, like Kelly, can see and go farther, then at least in my mind, I've left the world a better place than when I entered it, which is as much as anyone can hope for.

A Lifetime of Mentoring

Perhaps the best example I've ever encountered of what mentoring is all about is a man who spent a lifetime both mentoring and being mentored. And what a lifetime it was! For when the legendary John Wooden left this world on June 4, 2010, he was just four months shy of his one hundredth birthday.

His name is among the most famous in the history of American basketball, in which he starred, first as a player and then as a coach. Beginning at age 14, he led his high school team to the state championship finals three years in a row and was named to the all-state team all three years. Then at Purdue University, he played a key role in that team's national championship, and was the first player to be chosen as a consensus All-American for three straight years.

After earning a degree in English, Wooden taught and coached at the high school level, while playing professional basketball. After serving in the U.S. Navy during World War II, he returned to coaching and teaching. Then, in 1948, he was named the head coach of the UCLA basketball team, which would go on to heights never before seen in college basketball, and setting records which still stand. By the time he retired in 1975, his team had won 10 national championships in a 12-year period, including seven in a row. During four of those seasons, its record was a perfect 31-0, and, at one point, had won 88 straight games.

Following his retirement, he would live another 35 years, a period during which he made perhaps his most significant and important contributions. During most of those years, he made himself available to anyone who wanted to meet with him and seek his counsel. His "office" was a booth in a Southern California diner.

In an article in the August/September 2008 issue of *SUCCESS* magazine, author Don Yaeger described it this way: "Almost every day of the week, Wooden makes his way through those doors… and almost every day, someone is waiting for him. To the people who come to see him, Wooden is more than a coach—he is a mentor and a teacher…"

Wooden told his interviewer: "Mentoring is your true legacy. It is the greatest inheritance you can give to others. And it should never end. It is why you should get up every day." He also spoke of the importance of being mentored. "It is our responsibility," he said, "to be willing to allow our lives and our minds to be touched, molded and strengthened by the people who surround us."

A Touch on the Shoulder

Dudley Henrique was a troubled teenager who had shown absolutely no interest in any sort of positive mentoring relationship, or in being "touched, molded and strengthened" by anyone. His early life hadn't been easy, and the authority figures in his life had shown him no kindness nor any interest in mentoring him. It's unlikely he would have even known what the word "mentor" meant.

Born in 1937, during the worst of the Great Depression, he was six when his parents divorced. Then his mother married a hot-tempered man who had little use for Dudley and beat him severely and often. Two years later his grandmother took him to live with her in Wilmington, Delaware. He never saw his mother – or that stepfather – again.

For eight years, he lived with his grandmother, a working woman who had little time to mentor him. Not surprisingly, he often got into trouble and, at 15, was kicked out of school. His grandmother then sent him to a military academy that specialized in "problem" children. Within a year, he was expelled again and was back on the streets of Wilmington. He was 16.

One day, on impulse, he took a bus ride to nearby New Castle Air Base, home to the Delaware Air National Guard. There, in a hangar, he got his first close-up look at an airplane. "It was a World War II P51 Mustang fighter," he wrote. "I was hypnotized!" After walking all the way around the plane, he climbed up on the wing and into the cockpit.

When a guard spotted him, he yelled at him to get down. Dudley was scared and started to obey when he felt a hand on his shoulder gently pushing him back into the cockpit. Turning, he saw an Air Force captain wearing a flight suit. His name was James R. Shotwell, Jr. but, reported Dudley, "by the time I left the field that day he had become 'Jim.'" Jim Shotwell would be the first man to show a bit of kindness to him.

During the months that followed, Shotwell spent many hours with the troubled teenager, mentoring him, introducing him to his Air Force comrades and encouraging him to turn his life around. But it didn't take. Her patience exhausted, his grandmother sent him to live with an aunt in Southern California. But Jim Shotwell wasn't about to give up and he wrote to Dudley often. "Those letters," he said, "brightened my days."

Then, on March 19, 1955, came the awful news that 33-year-old Shotwell had been killed when the engine of his plane quit and he crashed. He could have saved himself by ejecting, but was close to a populated area and refused to risk it. By the time he maneuvered to a safer place, it was too late to eject and he died on impact.

A Changed Life

Dudley, who'd been unwilling to change, was devastated. The only real friend he'd ever had, the only one who had treated him with so much kindness, was gone. But those seeds of kindness Jim Shotwell had planted in his mind began to take root. "I started to think of Jim," he wrote, "and the many things he had said to me. Instinctively, I was aware that something had changed. Now I knew where I was going in my life and what I would have to do to get there."

He spent the next four years in the Air Force and, after his discharge in 1959, went on to earn a pilot's license. Flying was now his life. He became a certified flight instructor and developed a talent in acrobatic flying. "By 1971," he wrote, "I had accumulated thousands of flying hours, flown more than a hundred air shows, and lectured all over the country to flight instructors learning the trade. During those years I flew just about everything, including some experimental and military aircraft."

Dudley Henrique retired from active flying in 1995, but his contributions to aviation have been by no means limited to his time in the air. He has written extensively on a wide range of aviation subjects, including flight simulation, air safety protocols, and the techniques of flying high performance aircraft. He has also donated countless hours to various organizations, including the Professional Race Pilots Association and the P51 Mustang Pilots Association, and he is a past president of the International Fighter Pilots Fellowship.

Jim Shotwell didn't live to see the results of his kindness but, in befriending and mentoring young Dudley Henrique, he set in motion a series of events that would cause a troubled teenager's life to change and to bear fruit in ways he could never have anticipated. As Dudley's mentor, Shotwell left behind what John Wooden would later describe as his "true legacy."

—————— FOOD FOR THOUGHT ——————

Helping others stand on your shoulders is one of the best feelings I know. I'm sure I get more out of it than the mentees, who "are forced" to endure some of my tales of misfortune – sometimes more than once! Additionally, I always learn a new perspective from those I mentor. This new vision helps me see beyond the horizon and allows me to change roles from teacher to student while showing my mentee the value gained and the joy derived from helping others.

—— IN OTHER WORDS ——

*A true mentoring relationship also works in both directions—
they learn about new ideas from you
just as you learn timeless wisdom from them.*

~ Scott Allen

*Too often we underestimate the power of a touch, a smile, a
kind word, a listening ear, an honest compliment,
or the smallest act of caring, all of which have the potential
to turn a life around.*

~ Leo Buscaglia

*If a child is to keep alive his inborn sense of wonder,
he needs the companionship of at least one adult
who can share it, rediscovering with him
the joy, excitement and mystery of the world we live in.*

~ Rachel Carson

*Practice only makes perfect if you're practicing
with good feedback and guidance. Practice with
the help and guidance of a good mentor, coach or teacher.
It will greatly improve your performance.*

~ John Chancellor

*Each of us has warmed our hands around a fire, and each of us
has the role to bring a log to that fire, keep that fire going. We
benefitted from fire, so now we should add to it.*

~ David Gergen

*A single act of kindness throws out roots in all directions, and
the roots spring up and make new trees. The greatest work that
kindness does to others is that it makes them kind themselves.*

~ Amelia Earhart

Mentoring is a brain to pick, an ear to listen,
and a push in the right direction.
~ John C. Crosby

The secret of mentoring in any field is to help a person get to
where he or she is willing to go.
~ Ted W. Engstrom

None of us got where we are solely by pulling ourselves up by
our bootstraps. We got here because somebody—a parent, a
teacher, an Ivy League crony, or a few nuns—bent down and
helped us pick up our boots.
~ Thurgood Marshall

A mentor is not a person who can do the work better than his
followers; he is a person who can get his followers to do the
work better than he can.
~ Fred Smith

Mentoring can happen at any time or place.
It is both something we receive and something we give.
This is not a job you turn on and off.
~ John Wooden

I think if you truly understand the meaning of mentoring,
you understand it is as important as parenting;
in fact it is just like parenting.
~ John Wooden

A Life of Learning

The more we focus on how much we already know,
the less open we are to learning more. Studies have consistently
shown that people with a growth mindset –
those open to new ideas, approaching life with a childlike
curiosity – will fare much better in life.
~ John Chancellor

What's the first word that pops into your mind when you hear the word *learning*? Maybe it's *education, school, teachers, exams,* or *homework.* Do you get mental images—unpleasant ones perhaps—of long days in a classroom?

I've certainly had my share of such memories. Despite spending a lot of my life in formal schooling, learning hasn't come easily to me. Struggling in school started at a young age. I remember crying on my way to kindergarten which, looking back, should have been an omen about what the next 13 years was going to involve.

In kindergarten, Sister Marie Emelda would make the boys kneel on the hard tile floor in the cloak room for prolonged periods if they were acting out. As if that wasn't enough, the kneeling was occasionally accompanied by a smack on the side of the head with her arthritic hand. To this day, I attribute my mental slowness to the repeated closed head injuries suffered under her cold war era Stalinesque tutelage.

In first grade I was moved (somewhat incredulously) to the "advanced" group of students, only to be unceremoniously returned to the dullard section a few weeks later when I couldn't handle the increased work load. In addition, I had to endure missing recess because I was forced to go to a speech therapist for 30 minutes a day. While everyone else was out playing on the monkey bars, I was saying things like, "The little lucky lizard named Larry likes lasagna, licorice and lentils" over and over. To this day, I hate two out of three of those foods! No, I'm not talking about the lizard.

The rest of grade school was more of the same: poor grades, inarticulate speech, and escalating physical abuse culminating in the seventh grade when a nun who was built like a middle linebacker knocked me back to the Stone Age during a "Religion and Marriage" class. Sister Goebbels, who was Nazi-like in her delivery and mannerisms, taught "Religion and Marriage," which was always immediately after attending Mass on Wednesdays. It was 9:37 a.m. when she let this one roll off her tongue: "Sex is a very beautiful thing only to be shared between a husband and wife." I raised my hand and when called upon, innocently asked, "How would you know?"

When I awoke in the Principal's office, my ears were ringing, my head was pounding, my watch had apparently stopped at the moment of impact and I had no recollection of the event. To this day, I'm still cognitively impaired. To this day, I am still cognitively impaired. Where were we? Oh yeah, education.

My grades in high school didn't improve much. OK, they didn't improve at all. I finished high school with a cumulative GPA of slightly over a "C" average, which left me in the bottom quartile of the 500 students in my graduating class. God only knows what happened to the other 125 students who shared in my "shallow end of the wading pool" educational accomplishments. For reasons I will never know, the year I graduated from high school was the same year Drake University decided to let 95 percent of the students who applied into their freshman class. Parenthetically, they never lowered their standards to that degree again.

In college, I finally found my educational footing. My best friend Barry wanted to go to law school and studied for long hours at a time. My girlfriend at the time, Carrie, was in the pharmacy program and studied just as hard. If I wanted to hang out with either of them, I figured I'd better start studying. After realizing I actually could do well, I started to want to do well.

Don't get me wrong, I had no study habits and little of the ground work necessary for college, so it didn't come easily. But for the first time in my life, I started to believe in myself and actually knew I could do it, if I put in the time and effort. I finished college with a fairly decent GPA, thanks to a great set of friends who encouraged me, and a dedicated group of professors who really cared about the students.

I applied to a number of medical schools and was ultimately accepted into The University of Health Sciences/The Chicago Medical School. Medical school was, at least for me, like drinking from a fire hose. The material I learned in the biochemistry and physiology courses I took in college took about one week to go through in medical school. I had great classmates, however, who shared notes freely and often studied together. So, despite the amount of material, the studying was for the most part fun and manageable.

After medical school came a residency in emergency medicine. After that, I made the decision to go back to school every 10 or so years. In the early 90s, I went back to Arizona State University for an MBA and then again in the early 2000s to law school. During the first semester of law school, I was told the Dean wanted to speak with me. I went to her office and started the conversation by thanking her for accepting me into the school. I'll never forget her response; "Well, it's always good to have a doctor around in case someone drops dead!" I started to laugh, until I realized she was actually serious!

Education for me has been life-altering. Not because of the letters after my name – they're the very least important – but because of the amazing people I've met along the way, the experiences I've had, and the lessons I've learned. Education opened my eyes to new ways of interpreting an old set of facts. It also made me much more tolerant of others and much less biased in my views.

At the end of the day, education opens doors and thus expands the paths and possibilities you may one day want to travel. When you figure out what you want to learn, the process changes from tedious to fascinating and from worthless to highly practical.

While There's Still Time

It's never too late to go back to school which nowadays, thanks to online courses, is easier to attend than ever. I've taken a number of online courses (I'm currently enrolled in three) and expect to continue learning as much as I can through this medium. Besides, the really great news about taking classes online is that the nuns can no longer hit me when I say something stupid!

But learning isn't limited to books or classrooms, teachers or tests. It goes on all the time, and everywhere. The world is your classroom and the opportunities to learn can last all your life. Some 2500 years ago, the famous Greek philosopher Socrates was quoted as saying, "A wise man knows he knows nothing." When you think about it, that's the best part of learning—the knowledge that there's still more to learn. How boring would life become if you knew everything you needed to know?

Making learning a lifelong habit will keep you young. Henry Ford, the legendary pioneer automaker, put it this way: "Anyone who stops learning is old, whether at 20 or 80. Anyone who keeps learning stays young. The greatest thing in life is to keep your mind young."

Opening the Door

What's the password that opens wide the door of learning? It's part of the "original equipment" installed in us by the manufacturer, and it becomes operative at birth. The answer, of course, is curiosity! From the time we're first able to speak, the question we seem to most often ask is *Why*. I drove my parent crazy simply asking *"Why?"*

Among the best features of curiosity is that it's the perfect antidote to boredom. The late actress Lillian Gish commented: "As long as you're curious, you will never be bored." Author and teacher Ellen Parr struck a similar note with these words: "The cure for boredom is curiosity. There is no cure for curiosity." And Mark Parker, CEO of Nike, offers this advice: "Be a sponge. Curiosity is life."

A Curious Character

Let me tell you about one man for whom curiosity was a way of life. He was born in New York City nearly a century ago. After earning his Bachelor of Science degree from the prestigious Massachusetts Institute of Technology in 1939, he moved on to Princeton University, where he earned his Ph.D. degree three years later.

As a leading physicist, he took on various assignments before settling in as a professor at the California Institute of Technology (Caltech). During a distinguished career that included winning a Nobel Prize in Physics and numerous other significant awards, he was described by the British publication *Physics Journal* as one of the ten greatest physicists of all time.

Based on that brief biography of this man, it would be easy to conclude that he was an egghead – a guy you probably wouldn't care to sit next to at a party. But that would be a mistake. There was quite a different side to Richard P. Feynman, who was known by many less as a scientist and more as a prankster and practical joker.

Early in his career, he was part of a team of experts, based at Los Alamos National Laboratory in New Mexico, whose mission was to develop the first atomic bomb. It seemed an unlikely setting for pulling practical jokes. Feynman, however, would amuse himself by picking the locks of cabinets containing top secret documents and leaving behind cryptic notes suggesting the presence of enemy agents. There was nothing sinister about his motives; he simply enjoyed the challenge.

At other times, he taught himself how to juggle, play bongo drums, paint, and learn other skills with seemingly little, if any, connection to his scientific endeavors. Asked what led him to venture into such widely different areas, Feynman said: "I was born not knowing and have only a little time to change that here and there."

In two books he wrote, Feynman would go on to describe his never-ending quest to learn. The first, *Surely You're Joking, Mr. Feynman,* was subtitled *Adventures of a Curious Character.* It was followed by, *What Do You Care What Other People Think?*, subtitled *Further Adventures of a Curious Character.*

In his teaching and writing, his message was clear: "Explore the world. Nearly everything is really interesting if you go into it deeply enough. Work as hard and as much as you want to on the things you like to do the best. Don't think about what you want to be, but what you want to do."

Feynman played an essential role on the Presidential Rogers Commission, which investigated the Challenger disaster. The commission which he led ultimately determined that the disaster was caused by an O-ring not properly sealing in unusually cold weather at the time of launch. He was particularly incensed that NASA downplayed the risk of failure when they recruited teacher Christa McAuliffe, writing, "For a successful technology, reality must take precedence over public relations, for nature cannot be fooled." His inclusion on this panel and the conclusions from its investigation are simply the byproducts of his very curious mind.

The Questions You Ask

An excellent way to learn, and to satisfy your curiosity, is to ask questions. A scientist named Martin Perl, who also won a Nobel Prize in Physics, credited much of his success to doing so.

In his autobiography, Perl described the importance his parents placed on his education. "Going to school," he wrote, "and working for good marks, indeed working for very good marks, was a serious business. My parents regarded school teachers as higher beings, as did many immigrants. School principals were gods to be worshiped but never seen by children or parents. Parents never visited the school to talk about the curriculum or to meet with their child's teacher."

Yet it was his mother who instilled in him perhaps the most important lesson of all. "Every day when I came home from school," he explained, "she asked me, 'So, Marty, did you ask any good questions today?'" It was that habit of asking questions that helped Perl become a successful and distinguished physicist.

Another profession where asking the right questions is essential is journalism. In fact, the first lesson journalism students typically learn is how to write what's called "the summary lead." It illustrates the importance of having the key facts of a news story appear in the opening (or "lead") paragraph. A good leading paragraph answers six questions, called "the Five Ws and One H."

Nearly a century ago, Rudyard Kipling, the famed British author and poet, paid tribute to these six questions poetically: "I keep six honest serving men / They taught me all I knew. / Their names are What and Why and When / and How and Where and Who."

While they remain important "serving men" in reporting the news, they can also be very effective tools to facilitate learning in almost every field of endeavor.

The Books You Read

Reading is another great way to continue the learning process. One of the most prominent fans of reading I've ever heard of was Charlie "Tremendous" Jones; I introduced you to him in Chapter 6. In addition to a highly successful speaking career that took him all around the world, Jones was the CEO of Executive Books, a company he founded in 1966. Books were his passion and everywhere he went he'd proclaim: "You're the same today as you'll be five years from now except for two things, the people you meet and the books you read."

Over the years, his company, renamed Tremendous Life Books, has had cumulative sales well in excess of $100 million. He personally gave away countless thousands of books. "I hand them out instead of business cards," he said. "People may throw cards away, but they're unlikely to do the same with books."

In a long-ago letter to a young grandson, he offered this advice:

A proper diet is good for your body and the best books are good for your mind. Your life will be determined by the people you associate with and the books you read. Many people you'll come to love will be met in books. Read biographies, autobiographies, and history. Your books will provide all the friends, mentors, role models and heroes you'll ever need.

About reading, his message to just about everyone he met was the same: "Don't read to be big, read to be down to earth. Don't read to be smart, read to be wise. Don't read to memorize, read to realize. Don't read to just learn, read to sometimes unlearn. Don't read a lot, read just enough to keep yourself curious and hungry, to learn more, to keep getting younger as you grow older."

There you have them—the keys to becoming a lifelong learner: being incurably curious, asking good questions, and reading good books.

—————— FOOD FOR THOUGHT ——————

The books I've read over the course of my life have inspired, challenged, and provided countless hours of entertainment and education. What's in your library says much about who you are today and who you'll become in the future. One book was instrumental in shaping many of my ideas: *To Kill a Mockingbird*. It is, at least to me, a social commentary on kindness and how to interact well within the world around you.

—————— IN OTHER WORDS ——————

Be curious always! For knowledge will not acquire you;
you must acquire it.
~ Sudie Back

You can teach a student a lesson for a day;
but if you can teach him to learn by creating curiosity, he will
continue the learning process as long as he lives.
~ Clay P. Bedford

The important thing is not to stop questioning. Curiosity has
its own reason for existing… Never lose a holy curiosity.
~ Albert Einstein

Anyone who stops learning is old, whether at twenty or eighty.
Anyone who keeps learning stays young.
The greatest thing in life is to keep your mind young.
~ Henry Ford

My idea of education is to unsettle the minds of the
young and inflame their intellects.
~ Robert M. Hutchins

*The beautiful thing about learning is
nobody can take it away from you.*

~ B.B. King

*Never be too big to ask questions,
never know too much to learn something new.*

~ Og Mandino

*Learn all your life – from your successes,
from your failures. When you hit a spell of trouble, ask,
'What is it trying to teach me?'*

~ Earl Nightingale

*I think, at a child's birth, if a mother could ask a
fairy godmother to endow it with the most useful gift,
that gift would be curiosity.*

~ Eleanor Roosevelt

*You can learn new things at any time in your life if you're
willing to be a beginner. If you actually learn to like being a
beginner, the whole world opens up to you.*

~ Barbara Sher

Education is not the filling of a pail, but the lighting of a fire.

~ William Butler Yeats

CHAPTER

Enthusiasm:
Reaching New Heights

Be so passionate about what you do that you can't wait to get
out of bed in the morning. Make it so that you can't wait for
the sun to shine just so you can get out there and do your thing.
~ Chris Gardner

In Chris Gardner's early life, there wasn't much for him to get excited about. His stepfather was abusive, his mother spent time in prison, and he and his siblings lived for several years in foster homes. During that period, he got to know some of his mother's brothers, one of whom, his Uncle Henry, became the father figure he needed so much. However, a year later, when Chris was nine, Henry drowned. At that tender age, he'd already been exposed to much of the world's ugliness: domestic abuse, violence, illiteracy, alcoholism, and fear.

As a young adult living in California, his problems continued. A marriage was soon followed by divorce. Then a new girlfriend came along and, a year later, gave birth to a son, Chris Gardner, Jr. Chris was thrilled at becoming a father, and was determined to avoid all the problems he'd experienced growing up. Then his girlfriend moved to the East Coast, taking their son with her.

After a four-year tour of duty in the U.S. Navy, Chris returned to California. In the meantime, his girlfriend had returned with their son and given Chris sole custody. He was thrilled to have his son back, and the added responsibility made him determined to succeed, and to break the cycle of abuse and violence he'd experienced growing up.

He took a low-paying job at a research lab as the first step in what he hoped would be a career in medicine. The next step was selling medical equipment, which ended shortly after a chance encounter with a wealthy stockbroker driving a red Ferrari. Gardner then set his sights on a career in that field and became a trainee at a major brokerage firm.

With little income to sustain them, Chris and his son became homeless. He found shelter for them wherever he could, in flophouses, motels, parks and even in a locked bathroom at a subway station. Their story would later be told in the award-winning film, *The Pursuit of Happyness*, with Will Smith playing the role of Chris.

Finally, it was Chris's determination and passion that turned the tide. After completing his trainee assignment, he received a full-time position with the firm. As his career began to flourish, he moved on to another brokerage firm, and then launched his own company. Today, he's a highly successful stockbroker, entrepreneur, motivational speaker, and multimillionaire philanthropist.

Looking back on all he had gone through, he told an interviewer: "The future was uncertain, absolutely, and there were many hurdles, twists, and turns to come, but as long as I kept moving forward, one foot in front of the other, the voices of fear and shame, the messages from those who wanted me to believe that I wasn't good enough, would be stilled."

The Electricity of Life

In my view, the word "passion" simply seems "enthusiasm, carried to the highest level." And one of my favorite definitions of enthusiasm came from a man named Gordon Parks. "Enthusiasm," he wrote, "is the electricity of life. How do you get it? You act enthusiastic until you make it a habit. Enthusiasm is natural; it is being alive, taking the initiative, seeing the importance of what you do, giving it dignity and making what you do important to yourself and to others."

What was it that made Gordon Parks an enthusiast? It certainly wasn't due to the conditions under which he was raised. Born in 1912, he was the youngest of fifteen children in a terribly poor black Kansas family. Conditions worsened when his mother died and, at age 14, he was sent to live with relatives. They soon kicked him out, however, and he was on his own. To support himself, he took on whatever job he could find. One was at "a gentleman's club," where he had access to its library, allowing him to fill some of the educational opportunities he'd lost after dropping out of school.

When the Great Depression began in 1929, the club closed and Gordon hopped a train to Chicago. It was there that, thanks to a previously unrecognized musical talent, he taught himself how to play the piano and was hired to do so in a brothel. Later, he found work as, among other jobs, a busboy, waiter, semipro basketball player, and big-band singer.

In his twenties, he happened to pick up a discarded magazine, and was intrigued by the photographs he saw in it. Visiting a pawnshop, he spent $12.50 for a used camera. When he took his first roll of film to a shop to be processed, the reaction from the store clerks was so enthusiastic that he decided on the spot to become a photographer. Thus began a successful career, which included twenty years as a photographer for *Life*, which was then among the nation's most popular magazines.

But Parks' accomplishments were by no means limited to photography. Turning again to his musical talents, he wrote the music for a ballet and composed a piano concerto. He wrote poems and a number of books, among them a novel titled *The Learning Tree*, based on his childhood memories. A movie based on the book was released in 1969 and was directed by him. It was the first time a Hollywood film was directed by an African-American.

His second film, *Shaft*, was released in 1971 and earned an Academy Award for one member of the cast. From then on, Parks would continue his activities in film, writing, and photography. In 1988, in recognition of his accomplishments, he was presented with the National Medal of Arts by President Ronald Reagan. Other honors continued to come his way, including more than forty honorary degrees from colleges and universities in the United States and Great Britain. For a one-time high school dropout, Gordon Parks had indeed come a long way.

Though only 14 when his mother died, he'd never forgotten the seed she'd planted that would grow and flourish, continuing to bear fruit right up until his death at age 93. "She would not allow me to complain," he once said, "about not accomplishing something because I was black. Her attitude was: 'If a white boy can do it, then you can do it, too – and do it better.'"

Balanced Optimism

Another word that's closely tied to passion/enthusiasm is "optimism," a word that fits me pretty well. I am an optimist, possibly to a fault, although not to the level of "the cockeyed optimist" sung about in the famous musical *South Pacific*. Nor am I in the same category as the guy in the old joke who, on opening a barn door to see horse manure piled from floor to ceiling, starts digging. His explanation: "With all this manure, there has to be a pony in here somewhere."

I'd say my sense of optimism is somewhat balanced by at least a bit of realism. This optimism allows me to approach challenges in a way that helps me look at them as opportunities, rather than as obstacles. However, I don't mean you should be like that kid in the barn, or a Pollyanna. Pollyanna, incidentally, was the name of the young heroine in the century-old book of the same name; she always managed to find some good in every situation, by playing what she called "The Glad Game."

Instead, you should be approaching challenges with the requisite diligence and concern. Despite this, you can always find a silver lining in almost every situation.

Here's why I'm optimistic. I've learned from experience that things generally work out. I also know I usually end up in a better place after they do. I always learn something and I like a challenge. Part of this is from my emergency medicine background. It goes back to this thought: no one is dying, so how bad could it be?

Note: there is a downside to perpetual blind optimism, though. It happens when you fail to recognize the danger from a large impediment or barrier because you're so busy discounting its importance and looking for the silver lining. However, don't swing so far that you fall victim to the Chicken Little (a/k/a Henny Penny) Syndrome, crying "the sky is falling" whenever you encounter some minor mishap

I work with a fantastic team of realists who have the ability to see both sides of the issue and who will occasionally focus on the negative side. I'm sure there are times when my perennially optimistic outlook drives them crazy. I know for a fact that attitude has driven at least one CFO to insanity (though I think he may have already been part way around the bend when he came on board – he had a riding crop mounted on the wall in the office).

Anyway, at one point of my business life, we were trying to grow the business with very little capital. In 1995 I had the brilliant (not really) idea to franchise the concept. After two years, I thought we had a pretty good operating model that could be reproducible in other markets.

While we were slugging it out trying to promote this concept, someone from the *Wall Street Journal* left a message for me to call him as soon as possible. I thought we were finally going to get some recognition for this – at the time – ground-breaking idea. After three days of phone tag, I finally reached him. "Dr. Shufeldt, it's great to finally get to speak with you. Would you like to increase your subscription from one year to two?"

Nevertheless, I remain optimistic.

It's Up to You

There's a world of difference between having an optimistic outlook and having a pessimistic one. Winston Churchill described that difference well: "The pessimist sees difficulty in every opportunity. The optimist sees the opportunity in every difficulty." He made his own attitude clear with these words: "For myself, I am an optimist — it does not seem to be of much use being anything else."

For Churchill, Britain's prime minister during its darkest days of World War II, it was that attitude, perhaps more than anything else, that served him and his people well. As the nightly Nazi bombings threatened his nation's very existence, it was Churchill's "Never give up" attitude that would help his countrymen not merely survive, but go on to defeat the enemy.

"What is our aim?" he asked. "I can answer with one word: Victory – victory at all costs, victory in spite of all terror, victory however long and hard the road may be; for without victory there is no survival." Under his inspiring leadership, victory was, indeed, finally attained.

What was it that made Churchill an optimist despite the terrible conditions he faced? He did the same thing every optimist does, and what you can do as well—he chose to be one! It's simply a matter of attitude and you control your attitude.

FOOD FOR THOUGHT

Here's the take-home: there are people whose day-to-day existence is worse than the worst day of our lives. Yet they soldier on and make the best of their conditions, their illness, their trials, and their suffering. If they can do this, day in and day out – how can the rest of us not approach life with "can do" enthusiasm, passion, and unyielding optimism?

─────────── **IN OTHER WORDS** ───────────

Knowledge is power, but enthusiasm pulls the switch.

~ Ivern Ball

Today is life – the only life you are sure of.
Make the most of today. Get interested in something.
Shake yourself awake. Develop a hobby. Let the winds of
enthusiasm sweep through you. Live today with gusto.

~ Dale Carnegie

Find something you're passionate about and
keep tremendously interested in it.

~ Julia Child

Get excited and enthusiastic about your own dream.
This excitement is like a forest fire—you can smell it, taste it,
and see it from a mile away.

~ Stephen Covey

Without passion and the excitement, energy and motivation
it creates, it's hard to be successful. Then it's just work.
And that's not fun. I've seen hundreds of people who have
turned their great ideas into millions. They all share
one common theme. They have passion about what they
are doing. In that sense, they are doing what they love.

~ Donny Deutsch

Enthusiasm is the yeast that makes your hopes rise to the stars.
Enthusiasm is the sparkle in your eyes,
the swing in your gait, the grip of your hand, the irresistible
surge of will and energy to execute your ideas.

~ Henry Ford

Passion is not something you have to talk about. People feel it. They see it just as clearly as the color of your eyes, baby.

~ Chris Gardner

If you approach your work with optimism and a can-do spirit, your attitude, plus your aptitude, will determine your altitude.

~ Harvey Mackay

Those who are fired with an enthusiastic idea and who allow it to take hold and dominate their thoughts find that new worlds open for them. As long as enthusiasm holds out, so will new opportunities.

~ Norman Vincent Peale

Enthusiasm is contagious. Be a carrier!

~ Susan Rabin

Optimism is a happiness magnet. If you stay positive, good things and good people will be drawn to you.

~ Mary Lou Retton

You don't ever want to sleep when you're enthusiastic. If you can't wait to get up until tomorrow to get back to work on something, then you won't sleep much anyway.

~ Jim Trebig

Without passion, you have no energy —and without energy, you have nothing.

~ Donald Trump

Perspective: Look Again!

*By changing perspective and playing with our knowledge,
we can make the ordinary extraordinary and
the unusual commonplace.*

~ Roger von Oech

If I were to show you a picture of a horse and rider, on which the rider is facing the horse's tail rather than its head, the first question you're likely to ask is this: "Why is the rider facing backward?" That question is based solely on your *perspective,* when in fact it could actually be the horse that's facing backward.

The word *perspective,* in this case, is defined as: "a particular attitude toward or way of regarding something; a point of view." It's an important word; life is all about perspective. I consider that the most important of all the lessons I've learned. Simply changing your perspective changes everything.

For example, I recently had a patient who was in moderate respiratory distress from the pulmonary embolism (blood clot in the lung) we diagnosed in the emergency department. He was also dying of colon cancer. When I told him about his pulmonary embolism, he said,

"Whew, I thought it was going to be something really bad! At least I'm still on the right side of the turf."

For most of us – me included – the thought of a pulmonary embolism would be horrifying. But this man was afraid his colon cancer had metastasized to his lungs, so he was actually relieved when he heard the diagnosis.

Changing your perspective changes your attitude toward whatever life can throw at you. When all else fails to fix the problem, change your perspective.

The Prison of Familiarity!

I introduced this chapter with a quote by a man named Roger von Oech. I've long been a huge fan of his work. He's the president of Creative Think, which he founded in 1976, dedicated to stimulating creativity and innovation. He's the author of three best-selling books: *A Whack on the Side of the Head*; *A Kick in the Seat of the Pants*; and *Expect the Unexpected*.

He also designed a unique deck of cards called The Creative Whack Pack, comprised of sixty-four illustrated cards, describing strategies to get your creative juices flowing, and to help you view things from a different perspective. Recently, von Oech introduced a Creative Whack Pack iPhone app, which has been expanded to eighty-four cards.

On the first card, titled *Give Yourself a Whack on the Side of the Head*, von Oech explains: "The more often you do something in the same way, the more difficult it is to think about doing it any other way. Break out of this 'prison of familiarity' by disrupting your habitual thought patterns."

At the end of each card, he asks a question. A few samples:

- How can you whack your thinking?

- What are you curious about?

- What random ideas can you try?

- What would a six-year-old see if he were looking at your project?

- What off-beat "what if" questions can you ask?

- What can you eliminate?

- What's your blind spot?

A Detached Perspective

John Berendt is an American journalist and author whose non-fiction book, *Midnight in the Garden of Good and Evil*, was an immediate success, spending an unprecedented 216 weeks on the *The New York Times* bestseller list. Early in his career, he developed a fascination with the city of Savannah, Georgia, which is the subject of *Midnight*, and he eventually moved there.

Wanting to be sure he got it right, minus the pressure of deadlines, he worked without a contract and spent seven years on the manuscript. When his literary agent rejected it without submitting it to any publishers, Berendt was undeterred. He found another agent, who immediately submitted it to five publishers, all of whom made offers. The book was later made into a movie, directed by Clint Eastwood

Asked about his success, Berendt told a Barnes & Noble interviewer:

> *"When I'm writing, I like to gain distance from my work so I can tell how it will strike a reader who is seeing it for the first time. I do this through a trick I devised while I was living in Savannah writing* Midnight *— I would call my apartment in New York, the answering machine would pick up, I'd read the page of text I'd just written, then I'd hang up. A minute later, I'd call my apartment again and listen to the "message." Hearing my own voice reading the page over the phone — my voice having traveled 1,800 miles (900 each way) — gave me just the detached perspective I needed."*

Rule 13

One day, I came across a written list titled "The Golden Rules of Living." There were fifteen "rules" in all, most of which make sense: #1) If you open it, close it; #6) If you borrow it, return it; #7) If you value it, take care of it.

But there was one I have a real problem with: Rule 13. It's probably the most often quoted one in the bunch. No doubt you've heard it: "If it ain't broke, don't fix it."

Wrong! Crazy wrong! That's one of the warning signs of what I call "forced conformity." Here are some of the others:

- We tried it once and it didn't work.

- We've never done it that way.

- It's never been tried before.

- We've always done it this way.

- Don't rock the boat.

- Or the one said most often to me: "Were your parent's first cousins?"

Fifty years ago, the idea of man walking on the moon was preposterous. And who would have ever believed we could retrieve data from almost anywhere on earth, using a little machine on our laps – or an even smaller one in our pockets, or on our wrists. Indeed, we'd still be living in the Dark Ages if everyone slavishly followed Rule 13.

There's always going to be a better way – a smarter way – an easier way – a faster way – a different way – a more useful way – a more creative way – a more profitable way. It's all about perspective!

There's no satisfaction, no reward, in living by Rule 13. If it ain't broke, go ahead and break it, and come up with a better way to put it back together. Don't just accept things as they are. Ask questions: Why is it that way? How can we improve it? What other applications can we find for it?

You'll be amazed at what you can accomplish by allowing your creative instincts to take over. And don't ever say: "But I'm not very creative." Nonsense! That's the same as saying: "But I'm not very human." Creativity is part of our DNA. Authors and family counselors Evelyn and Sylvanus Duvall said it this way: "A child at birth has the capacity to become original. Or you can put him in a mold so that he will come out like everybody else." Or, as Pablo Picasso said, "It took me four years to paint like Raphael, but a lifetime to paint like a child."

Don't let anyone else squeeze you into a mold. Creativity is *not* synonymous with artistic ability. Artists display their creative side in their craft. Perhaps you can't sing, or paint a picture, or sculpt a statue, but you're every bit as creative, by your very nature, as those who can.

Find something that isn't broken – and break it! Follow the advice of a man named Jasper Johns: "Take an object. Do something to it. Do something else to it." Figure out how you can fix it, change it, improve it. You might be surprised at how creative you can be.

The T-shirt Perspective

The object Peter Shankman decided to focus on was titanic – or, more accurately, *Titanic*. The giant ocean liner was on its maiden voyage in 1912 when it struck an iceberg and sank, taking the lives of more than fifteen hundred passengers and crew. Of course, it made headlines all over the world but, as the years and then the decades passed, interest in it gradually faded.

Then, in 1985, seventy-three years after the tragedy, the wreckage was finally discovered, reawakening the worldwide fascination with it. A decade later, it was further fueled when filmmaker James Cameron started filming the wreck, as a first step in what was planned to be the partially fictionalized story of the ship, its passengers and crew, and of the survivors. Released in 1997, the film was wildly successful, earning fourteen Academy Award nominations and receiving eleven of them, including those for Best Picture and Best Director. To date, it has earned more than $2 billion.

Oh, Peter Shankman's role? Well, he's an author, entrepreneur, speaker, and worldwide networking expert. He's the founder and CEO of The Geek Factory, Inc., a social media, marketing and PR strategy firm based in New York City. He's written three books, but is best known for founding Help a Reporter Out, or HARO, which in less than a year became the standard for thousands of journalists facing deadlines and needing sources. HARO offers them more than 200,000 sources around the world looking to be quoted in the media.

Clearly, he's a very creative guy, but what was his involvement with *Titanic*? Well, he had nothing to do with discovering it, filming it, or promoting it in any way. He had a different approach – an entirely different perspective. He described it in the October 2013 issue of *Reader's Digest*.

> *"I was working at AOL in the 1990s when the company let go of 300 people. I was one of them. The movie* Titanic *was coming out, so I took my rent money and had 500 T-shirts printed that read, 'It sank. Get over it.' If I didn't sell those shirts, I was homeless. I sold 500 shirts in six hours and made five grand [$5,000]. Then I called* USA Today *and gave a reporter the story. I sold 10,000 shirts on the Web over the next two months and ultimately racked up 100 grand [$100,000]. That was my very first company."*

Shankman simply looked at the current event (the movie premiere) and the history event (the sinking) in a different, creative way.

The Nametag Guy

Nametags! They're everywhere. Police officers, firefighters, doctors, retail clerks, military personnel, church members, and business men and women all wear them. Go to a business meeting or social gathering and there'll invariably be a table at the door stacked with Sharpies and peel-off labels. I wish I had a dollar for every time I've written my name on one of them and stuck it on my shirt or jacket. I even have a few "permanent" ones issued by various organizations to which I belong.

Whatever the occasion, the tag usually comes off as soon as you leave the event you've attended. After all, you don't want to be seen in the checkout line at the grocery store, while you're still wearing that peel-off tag. Well, let me rephrase that. You don't want to be seen wearing that tag, unless you happen to be Scott Ginsburg. Scott has a much different perspective about nametags.

He's been wearing one now, 24/7, for more than 13 years. As I'm writing this, his website tells me the count is up to 4,865 days. He even has "HELLO, my name is Scott," tattooed on his chest! He had that done while *The Today Show* captured the event on film.

His story began in 2000. Eighteen-year-old Scott was leaving a college event one evening and, on a whim, decided to leave his nametag on. "It was one of those things I did just for fun," he said. "It was not a decision to put it on, but a decision not to take it off."

The next day, he met twenty new people. "It broke the ice," he says. "It gave people a reason to say 'Hello.'" That was just the beginning. Since that seemingly insignificant decision, he's become nationally known as "The Authority on Approachability," and has written a dozen books, including *HELLO, My Name Is Scott*, and his newest, *The Nametag Principle.*

"It has changed my life," says Ginsberg. "I've had conversations with thousands of people I'd never have met had I not been wearing my nametag. It's truly amazing how one small action can have such a profound and consistent effect on human behavior."

Among other things, he's appeared on virtually all the major TV outlets, become a much-in-demand speaker and consultant, was featured on *Ripley's Believe It or Not*, and in 2008 was selected "The Young Entrepreneur of the Year" by *The Saint Louis Small Business Monthly.*

I'd call that a rather impressive record, one that began with an 18-year-old student, a paper nametag, and a whim!

—————— FOOD FOR THOUGHT ——————

To me, education equals perspective and perspective equals happiness. The more I learn, the more perspective I gain and the less I'm satisfied with the status quo. Perspective has allowed me to look at the world and my place in it in a new light, with a whole new set of lenses. These new lenses have opened up countless opportunities. Where I once was blind, I now choose to see. My adventures in this whole new world give me great joy and happiness.

So, if you want to be happy, change your perspective. If you want to read a a great book on perspective, read *Unbroken*, the amazing story of Louis Zamperini. You'll never again lose sight of how fortunate and blessed you are. (I'll tell you more about him in the next chapter.)

—————— IN OTHER WORDS ——————

Be brave enough to live life creatively.
The creative is the place where no one else has ever been.

~ Alan Alda

Make visible what, without you,
might perhaps never have been.

~ Robert Bresson

One good thing about being young is that
you are not experienced enough to know
you cannot possibly do the things you are doing.

~ Gene Brown

The young do not know enough to be prudent,
and therefore they attempt the impossible —
and achieve it, generation after generation.

~ Pearl Buck

Why not upset the apple cart?
If you don't, the apples will rot anyway.
~ Frank A. Clark

Change the way you look at things and
the things you look at change.
~ Wayne W. Dyer

Creative thinking may mean simply
the realization that there's no particular virtue in doing
things the way they've always been done.
~ Rudolf Flesch

There is nothing insignificant in the world.
It all depends on the point of view.
~ Johann von Goethe

Originality is simply a pair of fresh eyes.
~ Thomas W. Higginson

Never tell a young person that anything cannot be done.
God may have been waiting for centuries for somebody
ignorant enough of the impossible to do that very thing.
~ John Andrew Holmes

You don't reach in and duplicate yesterday,
you create tomorrow.
~ Charles Kaman

Creativity is not the finding of a thing,
but the making something out of it after it is found.
~ James Russell Lowell

You've gotta be original, because if you're like someone else,
what do they need you for?
~ Bernadette Peters

Guts? Or Buts?

As long as you're stuck on your BUT, you'll never go after
what you really want in life. You may be able to see
what you want, but it will always be just out of reach.
~ Sean Stephenson

Sean Stephenson was 17 years old when he began a career as a motivational speaker. Nearly two decades later, he's still doing it, not only all across the United States but in nearly a dozen other countries as well. Along the way, he earned a bachelor's degree at DePaul University, served in the White House as an intern during President Bill Clinton's administration, became a board-certified psychotherapist, and has written two books.

Now that strikes me as a pretty good track record for a young man in his mid-thirties, but it doesn't even begin to tell Sean's story. You see, he was born with osteogenesis imperfecta, a genetic disorder known as "brittle bone disorder." Nearly every bone in his body was broken during delivery, and his parents were told his death was imminent. Somehow, he survived, but the road he was to travel wouldn't be an easy one.

I have treated patients who are afflicted with osteogenesis imperfecta. It's a very painful condition that severely limits growth and mobility. Sean is three feet tall and permanently confined to a wheelchair. By the time he was 18, he had suffered more than two hundred bone fractures. Yet, he refused to indulge in self-pity or to let his physical condition slow him down. Today, he lifts weights, does pushups and other exercises, and hasn't suffered a broken bone in years.

After graduating from college in 2001, he published his first book, *How You(th) Can Succeed!: Transforming Dreams into Reality for Young Adults.* Its cover features a photo of Sean in his cap and gown, and a tribute by well-known motivational speaker Anthony Robbins. It reads: "Sean is an outrageous young man with great strategies for life." Robbins had become a role model and mentor for Sean and wrote the foreword to his second book, *Get Off Your "But": How to End Self-Sabotage and Stand Up for Yourself.*

Published in 2009, *Get Off Your But* is a self-help book that includes Sean's own story, plus other stories and several exercises readers can do as they read. In the Introduction, Sean writes: "I have been on an endless pursuit to wake people up—shake them if I have to, just to prove to them that they are capable of overcoming anything that might arise in their life. Sadly, sometimes it's nearly impossible to fight the greatest negative force on the planet: the size of one's BUT!"

A few years ago, Sean was featured in a TV documentary on The Biography Channel. Its title, appropriately, was *Three Foot Giant*. It's a fitting description of a young man who has the guts to keep setting and achieving his goals, no matter what obstacles may lie in his path. If you'd like to see him in action, there are several YouTube videos available.

A Girl Called "Skeeter"

Little Wilma's birth wasn't as traumatic as Sean's, but she'd arrived prematurely, weighing only four-and-a-half pounds; her chances of survival were slim. It was 1940 in the rural segregated South, and she was the twentieth of twenty-two children in a poverty-stricken family. Somehow, she survived, but she was a sickly child, stricken with a variety of illnesses, including scarlet fever, pneumonia, and then polio, which required her to wear leg braces. The doctors told her she would never be able to walk without them, and her future seemed bleak.

But she was a determined little girl. Her siblings took turns massaging her legs and her mother drove her 90 miles every week for therapy at a Nashville hospital. Later, she would say: "My doctors told me I would never walk again. My mother told me I would. I believed my mother."

When she was nine, she shed her braces and began walking hesitantly without them. Soon after, she was not only walking, but running. She began playing basketball and ran around the court so fast that her coach began calling her "Skeeter." It was the first of what would become a series of nicknames given to her because of her running abilities.

Skeeter ran so fast that, while still in high school, she attracted the attention of Ed Temple, the track coach at Tennessee State University, and, while basketball was her first love, she began to take running more seriously. At age 16, a mere seven years since she'd shed her braces, she not only qualified for the 1956 Olympic Games, in Melbourne, Australia, but returned home wearing the bronze medal she'd won as a member of the sprint relay team.

It was certainly an amazing achievement, but Wilma Rudolph was just getting started. After graduating from high school, she enrolled at Tennessee State, where she became a start sprinter on the track team. She also set her sights on the 1960 Olympics, to be held in Rome, and it was there that she would reach new heights. She began by winning the gold medal in the 100-meter dash, and followed it by winning the 200-meter dash, setting a new Olympic record in the process. Finally, she earned a third gold medal as a member of the world-record-setting relay team.

This once sickly child, told she would never walk, thus became the first American woman to ever win three gold medals in a single Olympics. Nicknamed "The Black Gazelle" and "The Black Pearl," Wilma Rudolph became a worldwide celebrity, acclaimed as "the world's fastest woman," and was named "Female Athlete of the Year" by The Associated Press.

Like Sean Stephenson, Wilma Rudolph refused to let the obstacles she faced stop her from achieving her goals. "I ran and ran and ran every day," she said, "and I acquired this sense of determination, this sense of spirit that I would never, never give up, no matter what else happened." Asked what she considered the secret of "gutting it out" in the face of difficulties and setbacks, she said: " Winning is great, sure, but if you are really going to do something in life, the secret is learning how to lose. Nobody goes undefeated all the time. If you can pick up after a crushing defeat, and go on to win again, you are going to be a champion someday."

My Own Track "Career"

In high school, I wasn't built to run. In fact, I'm still not. That, however, didn't stop my track coach, during freshman year in high school, from entering me in the one-mile event. In many respects, who could blame him? The high jumper had just outjumped me, despite the fact I was using a long pole-vault pole, and the coach probably figured the best way to gracefully make me quit was to run me to death. Little did he know that I'd previously quit one thing in my life (the football team in 7th grade) and vowed never to quit anything again.

So there I stood, waiting for the gun to go off, signaling the start of the race. I eyed my competition. Many of them simply "looked fast." I felt like a yellow school bus lining up with a bunch of Ferraris. The gun sounded and the pack took off at a fast pace. Well, most of the pack. I was about 200 yards behind the next slowest runner who I believe may have suffered from polio.

The kid in the lead looked like a gazelle – he had cool lightweight shoes, short nylon shorts, a fitted running top and low-cut socks. He may have even had a headband. I was convinced his feet didn't even touch the ground as glided around the turns. Then, toward the end of the second lap, from my position at the rear of the pack, I could see the entire race unfold in front of me. It was clear that the tide had turned for the well-dressed gazelle.

While running down the straightaway, although it may have been delusions caused by hypoxia, I thought I heard a few people shout "Go, John! As I staggered by the stands for the start of the third lap, I was convinced I heard a few people shout, "Go, John!" However, by that point, I was so dazed from oxygen starvation to my brain that they may have yelled, "I have to go to the John," as they ran around looking for a port-a-potty.

Anyway, I started to notice that the gazelle was slowly but surely being passed by everyone. On the final lap, he was only about a football field ahead of me. It was go time! For the last 220 yards, I turned up the pressure to pass him. With lungs burning and legs of rubber, I finally caught up to him and as I started to pass him, he looked at me and whined; "Don't pass me, man, don't pass me!" But whether because of my Herculean effort or my massive nose, I managed to beat him by a nose at the finish – thank God, I have a big nose!

Other than the obvious about my lack of running ability, I learned a few things from this episode. Those who look the best and act the coolest are not always what they seem; often, they're just the opposite. Going out fast doesn't always mean you'll finish first. Sometimes, it may mean you'll finish last. If you just continue to gut it out, you'll not only finish the race, you may even pass a few contenders along the way. And finally, if you do get passed towards the end, at least have the courage to take it without whining.

The Torrance Tornado

I have one more story to tell you that also began on the running track.

It's about a man named Louis Zamperini, born in 1917 in Olean, New York to Italian immigrant parents. Two years later, the family moved to Torrance in Southern California. Unable to speak English, he became the target of bullies, so his father taught him how to box. He proved to be a quick learner and would later say: "I was so good at it that I started relishing the idea of getting even. I was sort of addicted to it."

To keep him out of trouble, his older brother Pete persuaded him to try out for the high school track team. As with boxing, he took to it quickly and well, earning the nickname "Torrance Tornado." At age 17, he set the world interscholastic record in the mile run. His ability resulted in a scholarship to the University of Southern California and, in 1936, at age 19, he qualified for the 1936 Olympics in Berlin. His roommates during those Olympics included the great Jesse Owens.

The U.S. team had traveled to Germany aboard ship and Zamperini, from a poor family and in the middle of the Great Depression, spent most of his time eating the free food. By the time the ship docked, he'd gained fourteen pounds. Entered in the 5,000-meter event, he finished in eighth place but it was during that race that a light came on. He recalled something Owens had said to him: "Run your guts out. It's one minute of pain for a lifetime of glory." He ran that last lap in an astonishing 56 seconds. Two years later, he set a national collegiate mile record, one that would last for seventeen years.

In 1941, as World War II was beginning, Zamperini joined the U.S. Army Air Corps, and became a bombardier. On one mission, his plane crashed at sea and, of the 11 men on board, only Zamperini and one other crew member would survive. For the next 47 days, they somehow survived, as their raft drifted deeper and deeper into Japanese territory. They were captured and would spend more than two years as prisoners of war, under brutal and inhumane conditions.

After the crash, Zamperini he was officially listed as "missing at sea," and a year and a day later as "killed in action." When the war ended, he returned home and was welcomed as a hero. In 1946, he was married, but his ordeal had scarred him deeply and he became, in his own words, "a hopeless drunk." Most nights, he was awakened by nightmares, and was consumed with hatred for those who had beaten and tortured him.

Finally, his wife Cynthia persuaded him to attend a Billy Graham Crusade. Graham's message that night was on forgiveness and Zamperini took it to heart. "I knew I was through getting drunk," he said. "That was 1949 and I haven't had a nightmare since."

Determined to confront his tormentors and personally forgive them, he traveled to Japan in 1950, where he met many of them, hugging them and expressing his forgiveness. In 1998, the then 81-year-old Zamperini returned to Japan, where he helped carry the torch for that year's Winter Olympics in Nagano. The telecast of that event included a 45-minute documentary about Zamperini, which reawakened interest in his amazing story. It became the subject of *Unbroken*, the well-documented and spellbinding story of his life, by Pulitzer Prize-winning author Laura Hillenbrand.

As I write this, *Unbroken* is being made into a movie, directed by none other than Hollywood star Angelina Jolie. Recently asked if he'd be in the film, Zamperini said: "only if I can play Angelina's boyfriend."

At 96, Louie Zamperini continues to share his story, in a good-natured and humorous way. He recently told one audience what it was like "to come back from the dead." He still has a framed copy of his death certificate and jokes that he billed the U.S. Army for "travel pay," covering the 47 days he spent adrift at sea.

I learned innumerable lessons from his ordeal, the main one being: no matter how bad I think my day is, my worst day is a thousand times better than Louie Zamperini's best day when he was adrift at sea or while he was a prisoner of war. If you read his book, you'll never complain about anything again.

Asked what he would say to today's teenagers, he replied: "All I want to tell young people is that you're not going to be anything in life unless you learn to commit to a goal. You have to reach deep within yourself to see if you are willing to make the sacrifices."

──── FOOD FOR THOUGHT ────

"Having guts" is a state of mind. It's not about physical strength, it's simply about "will." Is what you're embarking upon worth the time and effort, and do you have the will to see it through?

Tenacity comes in all sizes. Never underestimate anyone because of their size, strength, perceived intelligence, sex or age.

──── IN OTHER WORDS ────

Guts are a combination of confidence, courage, conviction, strength of character, stick-to-itiveness, pugnaciousness, backbone, and intestinal fortitude. They are mandatory for anyone who wants to get to and stay at the top.

~ D.A. Benton

There's a lot of blood, sweat, and guts between dreams and success.

~ Paul "Bear" Bryant

When you feel in your gut what you are and then dynamically pursue it—don't back down and don't give up— then you're going to mystify a lot of folks.

~ Bob Dylan

If you greatly desire something, have the guts to stake everything on obtaining it.

~ Brendan Francis

*Gold medals aren't really made of gold. They're made of sweat,
determination, and a hard-to-find alloy called guts.*
~ Dan Gable

*True champions aren't always the ones that win,
but those with the most guts.*
~ Mia Hamm

*" lot of people run a race to see who is fastest. I run to see who
has the most guts, who can punish himself into an exhausting
pace, and then at the end, punish himself even more.*
~ Steve Prefontaine

*It doesn't matter what you're trying to accomplish.
It's all a matter of discipline.*
~ Wilma Rudolph

It takes guts to get out of the ruts.
~ Robert H. Schuller

*Anybody with a little guts and the desire to apply himself can
make it, he can make anything he wants to make of himself.*
~ Willie Shoemaker

*I'd made it this far and refused to give up because
all my life I had always finished the race.*
~ Louie Zamperini

Integrity: An Inside Job

*The most important element we put into any goal
or relationship is not what we say or what we do
or what we have, but who we are*

~ Stephen R. Covey

In the above statement, Stephen Covey, the best-selling author of *The Seven Habits of Highly Effective People*, is talking about integrity. Simply put, integrity is doing what you say and saying what you'll do. The term is derived from the Latin word *integer*, which means "whole or complete." When a person has integrity, he or she is believed to have an inner sense of "wholeness" derived from consistency of action and character. The characteristics or qualities that comprise integrity are often defined as truthfulness, honesty, consistency, morality, account-ability, responsibility and loyalty.

Integrity, then, is about who we *really* are. Stephen Fry, British writer, actor, and TV personality, defined it this way: "You are who you are when nobody's watching."

However, imagine how your integrity is tested with millions of people watching you on national television – that's what happened to a friend of mine in the 2011 NFL conference championship game. Billy

Cundiff is a study in contrasts. Quiet, introspective, thoughtful, and smart are not typical descriptors of a professional football player. Billy is anything but typical.

Billy was the the Baltimore Ravens kicker who missed a relatively short field goal which would have tied the game and sent the Ravens into overtime against the Patriots. According to Billy, this was a field goal he made thousands of times during his career.

After the game, as millions watched, Cundiff met the media and displayed remarkable integrity. "There's really no excuse for it. It just didn't go through." Actually, he could have made all sorts of excuses. The art of kicking is as much mental as it is physical.

Kickers go through a routine every set of downs, as they prepare for a possible field goal attempt. Billy's routine in this particular set was rushed, in large part due to a scoreboard malfunction at Gillette Stadium. With the play clock ticking down, he was forced to sprint onto the field and had to hurry his kick as the clock ran out the second the ball was snapped. He remarked he knew it was a miss the second the ball sailed away. A lot of things should and should not have happened, all which would have prevented the missed field goal. A simple timeout would have changed the outcome.

Although he honestly could have made all sorts of disclaimers, Billy made no excuses and blamed no one but himself. Whether your integrity is tested, when you're alone or like Billy, in front of millions, how you respond is highly predictive of your future success.

Dr. Kent Keith, an attorney, university president, author, and former YMCA executive, had a broader view, saying, in effect, that we are who we are whether anyone else is watching or not. "We need to be in the world," he said, "fully engaged in loving and helping people, and doing what we know is right and good and true. But we don't have to be of the world—we don't have to get caught up in the rat race, sacrificing what is most meaningful to us in order to achieve the symbols of success."

Keith is best known for a series of statements in a booklet he wrote aimed at high school student leaders. It was titled *The Silent Revolution: Dynamic Leadership in the Student Council*, and included what came to be called *The Paradoxical Commandments*:

- People are illogical, unreasonable, and self-centered. Love them anyway.

- If you do good, people will accuse you of selfish ulterior motives. Do good anyway.

- If you are successful, you will win false friends and true enemies. Succeed anyway.

- The good you do today will be forgotten tomorrow. Do good anyway.

- Honesty and frankness make you vulnerable. Be honest and frank anyway.

- The biggest men and women with the biggest ideas can be shot down by the smallest men and women with the smallest minds. Think big anyway.

- People favor underdogs but follow only top dogs. Fight for a few underdogs anyway.

- What you spend years building may be destroyed overnight. Build anyway.

- People really need help but may attack you if you do help them. Help people anyway.

- Give the world the best you have and you'll get kicked in the teeth. Give the world the best you have anyway.

Those statements became famous largely through a case of mistaken identity. No less a figure than Mother Teresa had posted a version of them on the wall of her orphanage in Calcutta, India. Read at her funeral, they were described as comprising a poem titled *Anyway,* written by Mother Teresa herself, although she herself had never claimed authorship.

What I found most amazing about these statements is that they were written not by Kent Keith, attorney-at-law, nor university president, nor YMCA executive, but when he was a 19-year-old college sophomore! To me, those three words – Do It Anyway – state clearly what integrity is all about.

Today's media are filled with stories that lead to the almost inevitable conclusion that integrity is sorely lacking in our nation, and around the world. From swindlers to pedophiles, identity thieves to drug-using athletes, from prevaricating politicians to philandering spouses, virtually every facet of society has been infected by predators preying on innocent victims.

While integrity today seems to be lacking to a greater degree than ever before, we should keep in mind that it's been going on throughout recorded history – the story of Adam and Eve comes to mind.

Before we throw in the towel, however, let's look at some examples which indicate that integrity is still alive and well in many circles.

"Because that's what we do."

Over the years, the one sport which has seemed to avoid most of the scandals which have plagued other sports is golf. Now, I'm not talking about the personal lives of prominent golfers, but about how the sport itself is played. For example, golf is the only popular sport in which there are no referees overseeing the action on the course; the players themselves are responsible for playing by the rules, and for penalizing themselves for any sort of violations of those rules, whether those violations are seen by others or not.

Imagine a baseball game without umpires, where each pitch would almost certainly trigger a heated debate between pitcher and batter. The games would go on endlessly. The golfer, by contrast, is his own official, responsible for following the rules – no mean feat, by the way, judging by the size and complexity of golf's official rule book.

Over the years, there have been widespread reports of golfers calling penalties on themselves, often for infractions of which no one else is aware. In addition to perhaps a one- or two-stroke penalty, the financial consequences can be enormous. That golfers will do it regularly is a testimony to the standards of integrity present on the golf course.

One of the most vivid recent infractions involved a British golfer named Brian Davis, who called a penalty on himself for an infraction he wasn't even certain he had committed. Nevertheless, he not only called attention to it, but insisted that TV replays be reviewed to decide the matter.

Davis, who was born in London in 1974, became a professional golfer in 1994. He played primarily on the European tour until 2006, when he decided to join the PGA tour here in the U.S. While he had won a couple of tournaments in Europe, he has yet to win a PGA event.

He came close to his first victory on American soil in 2010, when he sank a long putt on the 72nd hole of the Verizon Heritage Classic in Las Vegas to tie Jim Furyk for the lead, forcing a "sudden death" playoff. On the first playoff hole, Furyk was on the green with his second shot, while Davis' shot was in a hazard. After reaching the green on his next shot, Davis felt he might have inadvertently brushed a loose reed on his backswing, a two-stroke penalty.

No one, including Davis, saw it happen, but he called over an official and asked to have the shot replayed on a nearby TV camera. The real time review showed nothing, and Davis would have been well within his rights to continue play, but he insisted the shot be shown again in slow motion. Almost imperceptibly, it showed that his clubhead had barely brushed a reed, and hadn't impacted his swing in any way. However, that reed, or "a loose impediment" in golf terminology, had indeed moved, incurring a two-stroke penalty.

Davis immediately called that penalty on himself, ending the playoff, and resulting in a victory for Furyk. The difference in prize money between first and second place was $400,000! But Davis was quick to point out that a great deal more was at stake than the prize money. "No," he said. "It probably cost me more like $2 million. A win would've gotten me into the Masters. My endorsement bonuses would have kicked in. A win opens so many doors. . . . There's no price you could put on it. It cost me $400,000 on that Sunday. But how much did it really cost me? Who knows? Winning at the Verizon Heritage would've been awesome. Probably the hardest thing is knowing how much a win can possibly change your career."

Asked if he thought about all that before insisting on the review, he said, "No. I thought I saw something move and I wanted to check. Because that's what we do. That's what golfers do."

The late Grantland Rice was perhaps the most famous and well respected sportswriter of the first half of the 20th century. Golf was among his favorite sports and he once said: "Eighteen holes of match play will teach you more about your foe than eighteen years of dealing with him across a desk." That's a test of integrity Brian Davis would have easily passed.

An NFL Legend

To continue our sports theme, Wellington Mara never played even one minute of professional football but few, if any, men have ever had the impact on the National Football League (NFL) that he had. It was an impact that began in 1925 when he became a ball boy for the New York Giants – at the ripe old age of nine. (I'd be remiss if I failed to point out that getting the kind of job almost any kid would covet had something to do with the fact that his father, Timothy J. Mara, had just purchased the team.)

But family ties had little if anything to do with the record Wellington achieved during an 80-year career with the Giants that lasted until his death in 2005. At age 14, he became a co-owner of the team, along with his older brother Jack. He moved into a front office position after graduating from Fordham University, and held a variety of leadership posts with increasing responsibilities, until becoming president and co-CEO in 1995. Under his leadership, the Giants won six NFL titles and a number of conference and division championships.

But as significant as his impact was on the Giants' organization, it was far greater on the entire National Football League, leading it to the prominence and success it enjoys today. For example, it was he who agreed, more than forty years ago, to share with all the league's teams the millions of dollars in television revenues the Giants received by its presence in the nation's largest TV market. Many teams in smaller markets owe their success today, and perhaps their very existence, to his generosity and foresight. His many contributions were recognized by his election to the NFL Hall of Fame in 1997.

He not only earned the admiration and respect of his fellow owners and executives but of the players as well. On learning of his death, Gene Upshaw, executive director of the NFL Players Association, said: "Wellington Mara was a true pioneer who understood what it took to make the National Football League great. History will show that his vision, integrity and willingness to share with small-market clubs paved the way for economic success."

One former Giants' star, linebacker Lawrence Taylor, considered one of the greatest defensive players in league history, used his 1999 induction into the Hall of Fame to pay tribute to Mara for his help, during the worst times of his drug addiction, with these words: "He probably cared more about me as a person than he really should have."

After Mara's death, other tributes poured in. Ernie Accorsi, general manager of the Giants, described him as "the moral conscience of the National Football League." NFL commissioner Paul Tagliabue called him "a man of deep conviction who stood as a beacon of integrity." Arizona Cardinals' president Bill Bidwell said: "Every individual who shares in the league's success owes an enormous debt of gratitude to Wellington Mara. Professional accomplishments aside, I will remember him just as much for his unmatched integrity, character and class. It was a privilege to be a colleague of Wellington Mara, but an even greater honor to be his friend."

Note the use of one word again and again: integrity, integrity, integrity! Wellington Mara didn't have to reach out to a retired Lawrence Taylor – but he did it anyway. Nor did he have to agree to share his team's millions and millions of dollars in TV revenues with the other teams – but he did it anyway! For 80 years, Mara stood strong as a model of integrity, a man of impeccable reputation and character.

FOOD FOR THOUGHT

Earlier, I mentioned sportswriter Grantland Rice and his quote about how a round of golf reveals the character or the integrity of a player. What is probably Rice's most famous quote describes the ultimate measure of one's integrity, no matter what the field of endeavor he or she has chosen in life.

> *"For when the One Great Scorer comes*
> *To mark against your name,*
> *He writes—not that you won or lost*
> *—But how you played the Game."*

IN OTHER WORDS

There is no traffic congestion on the straight and narrow path.
~ Thomas R. Dewar

Integrity begins with a person being willing to be honest with himself.
~ Cort R. Flint

Integrity is what we do, what we say,
and what we say we do.

~ Don Galer

In matters of style, swim with the current;
in matters of principle, stand like a rock.

~ Thomas Jefferson

A reputation for integrity is your most valuable commodity.
If you try to put something over on someone,
it will come back to haunt you.

~ Victor Kiam

The measure of a man's real character is what he would do if he
knew he never would be found out.

~ Thomas Babington Macaulay

I am a big believer in the 'mirror test.' All that matters is if
you can look in the mirror and honestly tell the person you see
there, that you've done your best.

~ John McKay

Right is right, even if everyone is against it; and wrong is
wrong, even if everyone is for it.

~ William Penn

Once you lose your enthusiasm, you lose your integrity. And
once you lose your integrity, you're a con man.

~ Russ Reid

Character is doing the right thing when nobody's looking.
There are too many people who think that
the only thing that's right is to get by,
and the only thing that's wrong is to get caught.

~ J.C. Watts

People with integrity do what they say they are going to do.
Others have excuses.
~ Dr. Laura Schlessinger

Better keep yourself clean and bright; you are the window
through which you must see the world.
~ George Bernard Shaw

Be more concerned with your character than your reputation,
because your character is what you really are,
while your reputation is merely what others think you are.
~ John Wooden

The Power of Teamwork

No one can whistle a symphony.
It takes an orchestra to play it.
~ Halford E. Luccock

The very first concert I attended was an eight-hour music fest featuring Pablo Cruise, the Steve Miller Band, and the Eagles. It was held at Comiskey Park on the south side of Chicago during a Super Bowl of Rock Concert tour way back in 1978.

I know that's ancient history for you, but I bring it up because I had the opportunity recently to see the Eagles during their current tour. They opened with a song called *Seven Bridges Road.* If you haven't heard it, the first part is sung in perfect harmony, *a cappella,* by the four remaining band members. They have been singing this song together for ages and it shows. Their harmony sounded unbelievable.

Harmony in music, as in most areas of life, is vitally important. The word *harmony* has its origins in Greece, where it means "to fit together, to join." Another word for it is teamwork. No team can work effectively without it, whether it be in music, sports, business, medicine, or any other field of endeavor. As a practicing physician, I've seen countless examples of it. Simply put, success in medicine requires harmony among the team.

Having specialized in emergency medicine, let me draw on my experience in that field. Whether in the operating room, the emergency department, or the urgent care setting, patient safety and operational efficiency depend on the ability of a group of individuals to come together and perform as a team.

Typically, these teams don't have the longevity or shared experiences of the Eagles; however, despite their lack of practice, their performance has to be nearly flawless, given what's often at risk.

How does a team achieve harmony? The most obvious answer is to simply practice and work together. This is often difficult to achieve with the number of different individuals who make up a typical urgent care team.

It's an overused metaphor, but there truly is no "I" in team. When one of its members believes he or she is the linchpin holding the team together, it may be time to have a blunt discussion about teamwork.

This doesn't mean that one person isn't ultimately responsible for the care of the patient; typically, the provider is that person. However, "care" is provided by the entire team. There are multiple critical actions during every patient encounter which, if not correctly handled, can have significant negative impact.

The Eagles could miss a note or be off an occasional octave and no one would notice or care. Missing the fact that the patient's pulse on discharge was 120 because the team wasn't working well together, however, could lead to a catastrophe. One bad performer can completely kill any chance for harmony.

Think of it this way: If I was singing with the Eagles in place of Joe Walsh, the harmony would be completely destroyed. Although I know all the words, I'd be off key and sound like a castrated mule – ok, at least an old mule.

In varying degrees, harmony is important in whatever you're doing – on the athletic field, in the school band, singing in the choir, writing for your school paper, starting a business, or conducting a science experiment.

Share Top Billing

Collaboration is another ingredient in the "secret sauce" that makes for good teamwork. Sticking with the musical theme for the moment, I recently read an excellent piece in *SUCCESS* magazine (March 2012) titled *Slowhand's Success Secret*. Written by Mike Zimmerman, it describes how guitarist Eric Clapton has remained at the top of his game for nearly half a century – and still counting. Along the way, he acquired the nickname of "Slowhand," and I'll tell you about that shortly.

Zimmerman calls Clapton "one of the great collaborators," then proves his point by listing more than a dozen of the big names with whom Slowhand has performed (B.B. King, Bob Dylan, Tina Turner, Sheryl Crow and George Harrison – to name just a few.)

"Collaboration is an incredible asset," writes Zimmerman. "For one, it ratchets up your productivity." He ends his article with this advice: "Seek out more and more collaborations… This works in any office, in any business. Start with willingness, enthusiasm and an open mind. Talk with others who complement your talent. Kick around ideas. Encourage excellence. Share top billing. You may produce something indelible and become the person everyone wants to work with."

In case you're wondering, the nickname "Slowhand" has nothing to do with Clapton's music style. Unlike the typical guitarist who, instead of interrupting a performance, immediately reaches for a new instrument whenever a string breaks, Clapton will stop playing and repair the string right on stage. Early on, audiences began clapping slowly and rhythmically while he was doing so. Thus, a nickname was born.

The Size of the Team

How many individuals does it take to make a team? Well, the answer, of course, is "it depends." One dictionary defines a team as: "a number of persons associated together in work or activity." In sports, the number of team members depends on the particular sport being played, with specific numbers outlined in that sport's rule book. A football team, for example, might include ninety players or so, but only eleven can, and must, participate at any one time.

In other endeavors, the number of team members can vary widely. The minimum number is obviously two, but the size of the team required to put an American on the moon or send a rocket ship to Mars would run well into the thousands. Regardless of team size, its effectiveness depends on the degree of cooperation and collaboration between the members, and the level of harmony they achieve.

Tennis Anyone? (or Two?)

If you have brothers or sisters, I'm sure you're familiar with the term "sibling rivalry." It's certainly something I experienced during my growing up years. But examples abound of siblings who have managed to put rivalry aside and work smoothly as a team.

In this particular case, the siblings are identical twins, born in 1978. Michael Carl Bryan was the first to arrive, followed two minutes later by Robert Charles Bryan. Their parents, Kathy and Wayne, have long been involved with tennis, both as players and teachers, so it's not surprising that the twins developed both interest and skill in the sport at an early age, winning their first tournament, as a doubles team, at age six. At the junior level, their parents decided it was in the boys' best interests that they not compete against each other, and they soon began winning regularly as a team.

In college, Mike and Bob achieved tennis stardom in both singles and doubles. After turning professional, they continued competing in both formats. As a singles player, Bob Bryan's top world ranking was Number

116, while Mike's peak was Number 246. Did that signify that Bob was more than twice as good as his brother? Not at all. Because Mike had been subject to injury more often than Bob had, he'd simply had less opportunity to compete in top-level singles tournaments.

In 2003, the Bryans decided to basically quit playing singles and to focus on doubles. At that point, where might you think two players who never even got close to the top one hundred level in singles might rank as a doubles team? Top ten? No way! Top fifty? Don't think so! Top one hundred? That might happen – eventually!

Well, I can't think of a better example of the power of teamwork. In fact, when these two modestly ranked singles players decided to pack it in and stick with doubles, they were already the top ranked team in the world, and they continue to dominate as no other doubles team has ever done. Through December 31, 2013, they've held the top ranking in the world for 344 consecutive weeks. That's more than six-and-a-half *years* – and counting! They've won more Grand Slam events than any other doubles team in history, and are the only ones to hold all four major world titles at the same time.

Of the twenty-four matches they're played in Davis Cup competition, Mike and Bob Bryan won twenty of them. And they won the gold medal in the 2012 Olympic Games, held in London. A year later, they were back in London, where they won the doubles championship at fabled Wimbledon. Teamwork! It works!

A Spelling Lesson

I've long been an admirer of Harvey Mackay, a man I introduced to you back in Chapter 6, who has achieved success in several areas. He's a well-known and highly regarded motivational speaker and the author of several best-selling books, including: *Swim with the Sharks Without Being Eaten Alive; Beware the Naked Man Who Offers You His Shirt;* and his most recent book, *Use Your Head to Get Your Foot in the Door.* Together, his books have sold more than ten million copies worldwide.

The business he heads, Mackay Mitchell Envelope Company, is one of the world's largest and most successful envelope companies, producing about four billion envelopes annually. Along the way, he somehow finds time to write a weekly, nationally syndicated newspaper column, which is filled with sound advice on the key factors needed for success, both professionally and personally; I consider it a "must-read."

Among those factors is teamwork, which was the subject of a recent column (12/5/13), headlined "None of us is as good as all of us." In it, he tells the story of a project in which British scientists tracked the flight patterns of great white pelicans, to which the scientists had taped heart monitors. They found that, when flying in their familiar "V" formations, the birds' heartbeats were slower than when flying solo, and they had greater range when gliding.

Mackay wrote: "Working together, the birds were able to accomplish their migratory goals by expending less energy and being able to fly farther than when they are alone. It seems that there is a lesson here… The entire group benefits because less energy is required to perform the great task at hand."

Then he added: "In human terms, even the most seasoned pilots need a control tower and ground crew." As an experienced pilot, I can certainly testify to the accuracy and importance of that statement. Even while flying solo, traveling from one point to the next is a team effort. Everyone from the mechanics, to the ground crew, to the controllers in the tower and along your route of flight, have stake in the game.

Mackay went on to tell a story of a man whose goal was to build the perfect automobile. To accomplish it, he decided to select the finest components, regardless of manufacturer. So he acquired the finest engines, the finest brakes, the finest steering mechanisms, the finest wheels, etc. In all, he gathered more than five thousand parts but when he tried assembling them, he wound up, not with the perfect automobile, but with a non-working collection of incompatible pieces.

Mackay's conclusion: "It's the same with people. A team of people or things with a common objective and harmony can be superior to a group of individual 'all stars' any day."

Mackay ends each of his columns with a brief takeaway, called *"Mackay's Moral."* In this case, it was: *TEAM: Together Everyone Accomplishes More.*

——————— FOOD FOR THOUGHT ———————

History is replete with the amazing accomplishments of teams: Apollo 13, the survival and rescue of Captain Edwards, sequencing the human genome, and building the atomic bomb, all required near superhuman effort by remarkably focused teams. The ability to work in a team environment is crucial for success in any important endeavor.

——————— IN OTHER WORDS ———————

Cooperation is the thorough conviction that nobody can get there unless everybody gets there.

~ Virginia Burden

The important thing to recognize is that it takes a team, and the team ought to get credit for the wins and the losses. Successes have many fathers, failures have none.

~ Philip Caldwell

The nice thing about teamwork is that you always have others on your side.

~ Margaret Carty

You don't get harmony when everybody sings the same note.

~ Doug Floyd

Teamwork is the ability to work together toward

a common vision… It is the fuel that allows
common people to attain uncommon results.

~ Andrew Carnegie

I am a member of a team, and I rely on the team,
I defer to it and sacrifice for it, because the team,
not the individual, is the ultimate champion.

~ Mia Hamm

One thing I believe to the fullest is that
if you think and achieve as a team, the individual accolades
will take care of themselves. Talent wins games,
but teamwork and intelligence win championships.

~ Michael Jordan

If you're on a team that really functions as a team, and I have
been, it's something you can carry for the rest of your life.

~ Tom Lehman

Build for your team a feeling of oneness, of dependence on one
another and of strength to be derived by unity.

~ Vince Lombardi

We don't accomplish anything in this world alone. . . . and
whatever happens is the result of the whole tapestry of one's
life and all the weavings of individual threads from one to
another that creates something.

~ Sandra Day O'Connor

People acting together as a group can accomplish things which
no individual acting alone could ever hope to bring about."

~ Franklin Delano Roosevelt

*Unity is strength… when there is teamwork and
collaboration, wonderful things can be achieved.*
~ Mattie Stepanek

*You can do what I cannot do. I can do what you cannot do.
Together we can do great things.*
~ Mother Teresa

*The best teams in the world are the ones
that help people become better and achieve more than they ever
thought they could on their own.*
~ Dave Thomas

*Teams were important in America's history – wagon trains
conquered the West, men working together
on the assembly line in American industry conquered the
world, a successful national strategy and a lot of teamwork put
an American on the moon first.*
~ Lester C. Thurow

Intuition: Knowing Without Knowing Why

If we are to learn to improve the quality of the decisions we make, we need to accept the mysterious nature of our snap judgments. We need to respect the fact that it is possible to know without knowing why we know and accept that—sometimes—we're better off that way.

~ Malcolm Gladwell

I have lived, saved lives, lost lives, and nearly died myself either following or not following my gut. If there's one piece of advice I'd give other than to persevere, it would be to trust your gut.

I've kept people in the hospital for no other reason than my gut told me something was wrong. The last one was a patient in the Emergency Department, where I made a completely lucky, albeit life-saving diagnosis of a rare and often fatal condition called Boerhaave's Syndrome, brought on by extreme vomiting.

My patient was a young lady who had mild shoulder pain after vomiting. Her initial tests were normal, but something in my gut still bothered me. So I listened to it and ordered additional tests, which revealed that condition. Within hours, she was on a ventilator, on blood pressure support, and triple antibiotics. As I said, it was a lucky catch. I did what every other Emergency Medicine physician would do and the patient ultimately did fine – thankfully, I trusted my gut.

Malcolm Gladwell, whom I quoted above, is the author of several popular and best-selling non-fiction books, including *The Tipping Point: How Little Things Can Make a Big Difference; Blink: The Power of Thinking Without Thinking; Outliers: The Story of Success; What the Dog Saw: and Other Adventures;* and his newest book, *David and Goliath: Underdogs, Misfits, and the Art of Battling Giants.* Outliers was the inspiration for my first book, *Ingredients of Outliers: A Recipe for Personal Achievement,* as well as for the book you're now reading.

The words I quoted are from *Blink,* which a *Fortune* magazine reviewer described as: "A fascinating book that makes you see the world in a different way." A *New York Times* reviewer commented that: "Correctly applied, Gladwell's theories could be used . . . perhaps most important, to alter human behavior."

As you can see, I chose the words for the title of this chapter from the Gladwell quote. It struck a familiar note, because it echoed a statement made by a man named Gavin de Becker, whom I introduced to readers in my earlier book.

In his book, *The Gift of Fear: Survival Signals that Protect Us from Violence,* de Becker – an FBI profiler, security consultant, and presidential appointee – described, in a thorough and compelling manner, the importance of intuition as an early warning system when our safety and well-being are threatened. In it, he defined intuition as: "the journey from A to Z without stopping at any other letter along the way. It is knowing without knowing why."

Intuition, of course, can benefit us in both positive and negative situations. While de Becker's book focuses on its value as an early warning system – by raising red flags – Gladwell talks more about equally important reasons for us to pay attention to the signals our intuitions send our way, without the physical danger.

A Small Miracle

Gladwell ends *Blink* with a story that dramatically illustrates what can happen when we let our intuitions – rather than our prejudices, preconceived notions, and "knowledge" – lead us in the right direction. Until fairly recently, Gladwell reports, there were relatively few female musicians in classical music orchestras. This was especially true with such instruments as the trombone and French horn. Women, the theory went, lacked the strength and lung power to play those instruments well. Therefore, during the audition process, they stood little chance of selection.

Then something changed – the decision was made to conduct auditions in which candidates would perform behind screens, out of sight of the decision makers. Gladwell describes what happened next: "In the past thirty years, since screens became commonplace, the number of women in the top U.S. orchestras has increased fivefold."

One woman in particular, after easily winning her audition, brought gasps from those who had selected her when she stepped out from behind the screen. The biggest surprise wasn't her gender, but the fact that she had previously performed with this very orchestra as a substitute. "They *knew* her," Gladwell exclaimed, but: "Until they listened to her with just their ears, they had no idea she was so good." He described it as a small miracle, "the kind of small miracle that is always possible when we take charge of the first two seconds…" In other words, that's what can happen when we remove our preconceived notions and let our intuition be our guide.

Follow Your Heart

As a teenager, you may already found what you want to do with your life and have begun the journey. If so, congratulations! If not, I suggest you listen carefully to that little voice inside you – your intuition. There are probably many people in your life – your parents or other family members perhaps – who've been making suggestions, offering advice, etc., and most likely with the very best motives. By all means, listen carefully to them, but I hope you'll also pay attention to that little voice inside you – your intuition.

A colleague of mine recently told me his story. His earliest memories were of his mother reading to him, which she'd been doing from his infancy. That began a great love for reading and, by the time he'd finished high school, he'd decided to follow in the footsteps of his father, a successful newspaperman. In college, he majored in journalism, wrote for the school newspaper, and loved every minute of it.

After graduating, he was offered a job with a small suburban newspaper. At the same time, an uncle had suggested he consider a business career and arranged an interview with a friend who owned a property management company. That interview also brought a job offer – at more than double the salary and much better benefits than the newspaper job. He knew which way he really wanted to go, but decided to put aside his gut feeling and take the other job "for a couple of years," and then follow the leading of that small voice inside him.

The "couple of years" became ten and then twenty. They were successful years, culminating in his selection as president of the firm after his boss retired. Yet, despite his success, they'd been largely unfulfilling years, and he was ready for something different. By then in his mid-forties, he decided to go into business for himself as a management consultant. Then, in an interview with an established and successful consultant he'd just met, he happened to casually mention that he'd majored in journalism in college.

The consultant's response was immediate. "You majored in journalism," he exclaimed. "Do you think you could write an article about what my firm does?" Indeed, he wrote that article, which was just the first step in a new career that, to date, has led to more than three dozen books, plus countless articles and newsletters.

Does he ever wonder how things might have turned out if he'd paid attention to his intuition and taken the newspaper job? "I think about it once in awhile," he told me, "but I have no regrets. Even with the late start, it's been a great ride, and I plan to keep doing it as long as I can. I love words, but the word 'retirement' isn't even in my vocabulary."

I asked him what advice he might have for a young person today who's trying to decide which road to take. He pointed me to a quote by the late Steve Jobs, the creative genius who launched and later guided Apple to the preeminent position it enjoys in the world today. "Your work is going to fill a large part of your life," Jobs said, "and the only way to be truly satisfied is to do what you believe is great work. And the only way to do great work is to love what you do. If you haven't found it yet, keep looking. Don't settle."

FOOD FOR THOUGHT

If you're going to stand out, to become an Outlier, it's important to develop good relationships, to be a team player, a person of integrity and persistence, to recognize the value of mentoring and networking, and to develop the other qualities we've described in these pages. But don't ever lose sight of your uniqueness.

Musician, singer, songwriter and actor Jon Bon Jovi said it this way: "Each one of you has something no one else has, or ever had: your fingerprints, your brain, your heart. Be an individual. Be unique. Make someone notice."

I don't know who first said this, but it's worth repeating: "You were born an individual, don't die a copy." Let your intuition be your guide in becoming all you can be.

IN OTHER WORDS

Listen to your inner voice for it is a
deep and powerful source of wisdom, beauty and truth,
ever flowing through you. Learn to trust it,
trust your intuition, and in good time, answers to all you seek
to know will come, and the path will open before you.

~ Caroline Joy Adams

Intuition is always right in at least two important ways;
It is always in response to something.
It always has your best interest at heart.

~ Gavin de Becker

Your intuition is the pilot's seat of your soul.
If you don't trust it, you'll keep missing the most important
of destinations in life.

~ Kaiden Blake

None of us will ever accomplish anything excellent
or commanding except when he listens to this whisper
which is heard by him alone.

~ Ralph Waldo Emerson

Call intuition cosmic fishing.
You feel a nibble, then you've got to hook the fish.

~ R. Buckminster Fuller

The one thing that you have that nobody else has is you.
Your voice, your mind, your story, your vision. So write and
draw and build and play and dance and live as only you can.

~ Neil Gaiman

There can be as much value in the blink of an eye
as in months of rational analysis.

~ Malcolm Gladwell

Today you are you.
That is truer than true.
There is no one alive
that is youer than you."
~ Theodor [Dr.] Seuss Geisel

What another would have done as well as you, do not do it.
What another would have said as well as you, do not say it.
What another would have written as well, do not write it. Be
faithful to that which exists nowhere but in yourself —
and thus make yourself indispensable.
~ André Gide

I wanted only to try to live in accord with the promptings
which came from my true self. Why was that so very difficult?
~ Hermann Hesse

Cherish forever what makes you unique,
cuz you're really a yawn if it goes.
There can be as much value in the blink of an eye
as in months of rational analysis.
~ Bette Midler

Read, every day, something no one else is reading.
Think, every day, something no one else is thinking.
Do, every day, something no one else would be
silly enough to do. It is bad for the mind to continually be part
of unanimity. There can be as much value in the blink of an eye
as in months of rational analysis.
~ Christopher Morley

Remember always that you have not only the right to be an
individual, you have an obligation to be one. You cannot make
any useful contribution in life unless you do this.
~ Eleanor Roosevelt

Each of us is created in a unique way.
Our personalities are as diverse as the universe itself.
Yet there is one constant: We can, by using what we have to
the fullest, stand out from the crowd.
~ Glenn Van Ekeren

CONCLUSION

At some point in your life, maybe even today, you'll know everything in this book. None of it is rocket science and every one of us has the potential to excel in every trait discussed. However, most of us, me included, still struggle with many of these qualities. Nevertheless, and maybe thankfully, life should be a never-ending growth or evolutionary cycle.

So, don't expect perfection; the ideas and traits in this book can take years to master. Even the very best people you'll meet during the course of your life may occasionally struggle on seemingly basic concepts; people lose their temper, make egotistical remarks, give up, quit learning, lose their sense of humor or sense of themselves, and simply get lost on the path of their life. It happens to everyone at some point. When it happens to you, take a deep breath, regroup and move on along your path.

You already have the capacity to change the world; the tenacity to change the world is the easy part, provided you're passionate about the cause.

So, use this book to "stand on the shoulders of the giants" we've featured in these pages to look beyond your own personal horizon toward that amazing future.

I'll leave you with this bit of wisdom from Mark Twain:

> *"Twenty years from now you will be more disappointed by the things that you didn't do than by the ones you did do. So throw off the bowlines. Sail away from the safe harbor. Catch the trade winds in your sails. Explore. Dream. Discover."*

ACKNOWLEDGMENTS

This book has been a work in progress for years and would not have come to fruition without the help of a number of individuals to whom I am profoundly indebted.

Bob Kelly has had a profound influence on this project. He provided a wealth of information and anecdotes laced with his own personal experience. Without Bob's ability, work ethic, and diligence, this book could not have been completed.

Vickie Mullins from Mullins Creative helped shepherd the book through the design and production phase.

Slobodan Cedic whose creative design shines brightly on the cover.

ABOUT THE AUTHOR

John Shufeldt is a serial student, an indefatigable change agent and a multidisciplinary entrepreneur who has studied the traits and qualities of extraordinary individuals – outliers – for more than three decades. This is his second book in that field. The first, *Ingredients of Outliers,* was released in 2013.

John received his BA from Drake University in 1982 and his MD from the University of Health Sciences/ The Chicago Medical School in 1986. He completed his Emergency Medicine Residency at Christ Hospital and Medical Center in 1989 where he spent his final year as Chief Resident. John received his MBA in 1995, and his Juris Doctorate in 2005, both from Arizona State University. He is admitted to the State Bar in Arizona, the Federal District Court, and Supreme Court of the United States. His certifications include Fellow, American Board of Emergency Medicine, Fellow, College of Legal Medicine, and American College of Emergency Physicians.

He founded numerous health and non-health care businesses and continues to practice emergency medicine and law. He is the business manager and one of the founding partners of Empower Emergency Physicians and continues to practice emergency medicine at St. Joseph's Hospital and Medical Center. In 2010 John started MeMD, an on-demand virtual health care venture designed specifically to improve access to and reduce the cost of health care.

An avid rotor and fixed wing pilot, he holds a multi-engine Airline Transport Pilot rating and is type-rated in a North American T-28 and Citation 510. John has been actively involved in law enforcement as a "SWAT Doc" since 1998 and is currently Medical Director of the Phoenix Police SWAT team. He is Past President of the Board of the Men's Anti-violence Network, and serves on the Drake University Board of Trustees and the Sandra Day O'Conner College of Law Alumni Board.

John has authored and co-authored books on Children's Emergencies and Contract Issues for Emergency Medicine Physicians. He writes and lectures on a variety of subject matters to graduate medical, business and law students. He is the Health Law Editor and on the Advisory Board for the Journal of Urgent Care Medicine and was the Editor in Chief of *Urgent Care Alert* and *ED Legal Bulletin*.

He is an adjunct professor at the Arizona State University, W.P. Carey School of Business where he taught Health Law and Ethics to MBA and Health Sector Management students and is an adjunct professor at the Sandra Day O'Connor College of Law where he teaches a seminar on Health Law Entrepreneurism.

You can find more information about John and his work at: www.ingredientsofoutliers.com.

CPSIA information can be obtained
at www.ICGtesting.com
Printed in the USA
FFOW01n1441150314